Nobody's Perfect

By Sue M. Wilson

Open Door Publishing - Hendersonville NC

Published by Open Door Publishing - Hendersonville, NC
www.suemwilson.com
ISBN: 978-0-9991104-0-9

Library of Congress Control Number: 2018900389

This publication is not intended as a substitute for the advice of health care professionals.

Contents

Dedicated to my husband Len – I love our imperfect life, and the exciting adventures we continue to enjoy together…

Acknowledgments

I offer a heartfelt thanks to my launch team! You are an amazing group of friends, family and fellow members of Self-Publishing School! And most of all, I give thanks to my Lord Jesus Christ for the freedom that I now walk in.

So what if your life's going to be messy?
Perfect isn't the plan; purpose is.

~ Ann VosKamp

Life is messy!

The day held several errands for me, and I was relieved that most of them had been checked off my list! Just as I heard my stomach growl, I smiled because food was in sight. Making it through the drive-through in record time, I decided I could take a few extra minutes to enjoy my lunch. As I parked my car, I couldn't wait to take my first bite; unfortunately, as I did, I experienced a burrito blow out. Managing to clean up most of the mess, I sadly discovered some of that gooey goodness on my white shirt. With more clean-up required, I seemed to just be spreading the stain. Hmm . . . I thought to myself, if I zipped up my jacket I could cover up the stain. So that is what I did as I headed for my last stop.

My face began to flush, not only because I was feeling rushed. I was feeling hot with my jacket zipped up so far. Hoping to get what I needed from the grocery store as quickly as possible, I happily spotted the last item on my list and grabbed a carton of root beer. As I transferred the drink to my cart, one of the lids loosened just enough to create a fountain-like spray. The only thing I had to clean up the mess with was a few napkins stuffed in my jacket pocket from lunch. Unable to find a store employee for assistance, I managed to remove the leaky carton from my cart and set it down in the middle of the aisle without getting the sticky brew all over me. I carefully grabbed another carton of root beer and headed for the checkout.

"Excuse me; there is need for cleanup on aisle five," I said, interrupting the checker as he tried to ask me if I had found everything I needed. I was too hot and embarrassed to give him the details; I just wanted to get out of there!

Unloading the groceries from my car, I experienced the grand finale of mishaps for the day as one of the cans of root-beer fell out of the carton onto the garage floor, spraying all over me and the car. With another root beer clean-up necessary, and no one to report it to, all I could do was get that jacket off and clean up another mess — and enjoy a good laugh! I now had further proof of what I already suspected: life is messy - and there will always be a need for a clean-up, no matter what aisle you're on!

The reason I am telling you this story is to point out the best part: I could laugh! Smiles continued to spread across my face that day, every time I thought about the events it had held; actually, I'm smiling now as I write this too! This might not seem like a big deal to most, but to someone who struggles with perfectionism, it truly was!

I now realize that I wore the title of Perfectionist as though it were a badge of honor. I just thought I had high standards. Perhaps you can relate. As I began to understand what being a perfectionist really meant, I knew that was not what I want to be, or how I want to live life. I'm in recovery now, and I don't say that lightly; addictions are deadly. I have already wasted too many years of my life trying to be perfect - and I never want to feel that compulsion again!

My hope for you as you read this book is that you will no longer want to waste time trying to be - and trying to do - perfect! In the next chapter we will take a look at what perfectionism really is, and what it is not. Throughout the book we will also look at some common triggers that propelled me into perfectionism and at counteractive ways to disarm them! These triggers are not solely connected to perfectionism but overlap into other common struggles we can have. Although I wrote this book as a former perfectionist, you may also find it helpful in understanding the plight of perfectionists you know.

As you break free from perfectionism and its relentless ways, you will enjoy your imperfect life — which, by the way, is perfect (enough).

It's all Barbie's fault!

Before we get to that, I have a theory about how some of us started feeling like we needed to be perfect. It's all Barbie's fault! Barbie made her first appearance in 1959 and has been shaping the way many little girls viewed and have continued to view themselves ever since! I remember playing with my Barbie for hours on end. I dressed her in her amazing designer clothes, which I had to save my allowance for. Each outfit came with a perfect pair of little shoes that I more than once had to retrieve from the vacuum cleaner bag. She drove her perfect sports car to her very own Barbie Dream House that was — you guessed it - perfect.

Barbie's well-to-do lifestyle placed value on material things and got little girls thinking about things they shouldn't have to think about! Barbie's perfect image was especially hard on us flat-chested or overweight girls. We have more to learn about Barbie as we discover that even she is far from perfect! In all seriousness, some of us began at an early age to measure ourselves against something that was neither real nor wholesome. Unfortunately, many of us grew up thinking our bodies should look like Barbie's, causing our self-esteem to plummet.

It's not just how we look!

The way we look is not the only way perfectionism taunts us. There can be a lot of pressure on us because of the way our homes look too! Since the launching of television's HGTV, it's easy to feel discontented with the way our homes look. If you're like me, you can drool over the transformation taking place, home after home — and all in less than an hour! Intellectually I realize that it takes weeks, even months, to accomplish these alterations — and that with a team of workers! What I think mesmerizes the audience most is seeing the before and after. Tracking a project from start to finish is great fun (and a nice diversion from all the unfinished projects around me). Unfortunately, when the show is over, it's easy to feel discouraged and even depressed because we have been reminded that our homes are far from perfect!

There's more that we wish were perfect: how about a perfect marriage, or being a perfect parent with perfect children? And while we are at it, wouldn't we all like a perfect friend or two? A perfect job? You have got to be kidding me! We know perfection is not possible, but we still can long for these things.

You're not alone!

I think everyone of us has some perfectionist tendencies. We feel that we're not quite good enough. I had an opportunity to teach a workshop about perfectionism at a women's conference. I wondered if anyone would choose my workshop over the others that were offered because at that time I did not know if there were many women like me who struggled with perfectionism. I was surprised by the number of women who came! I taught the workshop twice, with seventy women in total attendance. I told you that you aren't alone!

During each workshop we took a "perfectionist test" as a class, with lots of hoots and hollers! (You will have the chance to take that same test in the next chapter, with a few additions from the group.) Just being together was comforting. So many times we can feel like we are the only ones struggling with such things. It was not a misery-loves-company thing but more a let's-conquer-this-thing-called-perfectionism — and start enjoying our imperfect lives!

At the beginning of the workshop I held a drawing for a few gifts to give away. After reading the name of the winner from the paper, I tossed it over my shoulder behind me. With several gifts to give away, there were several crumpled pieces of paper on the floor. I enjoyed watching some of the women squirm in their seats while I was doing this. After the drawing was over, I finally acknowledged my mess by asking if any of them were bothered by the papers on the floor. I did not ask them to raise their hands. I could tell that the mess did not bother all of them, so I knew that there were different degrees of perfectionist in the room. I left those crumpled papers on the floor throughout the class, hoping that did not distract anyone from my teaching! I had to chuckle when, at the end of class, a class participant picked up those papers (I actually had forgotten about them!) and put them in the trash before she left. This happened in both workshops — at least perfectionists are consistent!

More research required

Wanting to extend my research further, and suspecting that there were probably more perfectionists out there, I looked for some perfectionists I personally knew. We soon organized a group of women who agreed to meet at my home, one morning a week, for six weeks. These women honestly answered the questions that I had prepared and willingly shared their personal struggles with perfectionism. The transparency in the group was refreshing. Through both laughter and tears we all agreed that society encourages it in all the media. The chapters in this book were developed from the discussions I had each week with these wonderful women.

Are you ready to get to work?

So, are you ready to increase your quality of life and get busy really living? Are you ready to celebrate who you were meant to be? How about being ready to quit wasting time thinking about how you wished you looked or your home looked, or feeling that everything you do must be Pinterest-worthy? If you answered a yes to even one of these questions, this book was written for you! I hope you are ready to embark on an amazing journey!

Will this be easy? No. Will it be worth it? Yes! Don't live another day feeling like you're not enough, and don't waste another minute comparing yourself to someone else! Don't spend another second holding your personal bar so high that no one could reach it! Begin to discover and believe that your imperfect life is perfect enough — because it is!

CHAPTER 1

If you look for perfection, you'll never be content.

~ Leo Tolstoy

Perfectionism: What's the problem?

The Perfect move . . .

I fit into the category of learning things the hard way, but the good thing is, I'm learning! One of the things I have become quite proficient at during our many years of marriage is moving! Because we are builders, I have had plenty of opportunity to hone my skills!

Our first long-distance move, to Brisbane, Australia, held some new challenges for me, and I would need to pull out all of the stops and use keen strategy to execute this move of over 7,000 miles — perfectly!

First we needed to pack everything we owned into a container that would be shipped to Brisbane, our new home. Our load was lightened through making donations, sharing possessions with friends, shedding through yard sales, and selling the vehicles we would not be shipping. The container we were using was 20' long, 8' wide and 8' high; we were assured by the shipping company that everything would travel well from Los Angeles to Brisbane and with the least amount of damage if we packed the container tightly. Tight packing would keep the shifting to a minimum during the voyage across the Pacific Ocean.

Our container would not travel alone; there could be up to 15,000 containers on the same ship. Each container would be in a stack approximately 10 containers high. I also learned (not from the shipping company) that an estimated 10,000 containers are lost at sea every year, often through sliding into the ocean during a storm. The company recommended that we purchase insurance; unfortunately, that would double the price of the shipping. I thought we should buy the insurance, but my husband convinced me otherwise. He contended that we did not need the insurance because it was too expensive and, anyway, the odds were in our favor that nothing would happen to our particular container! I struggled to accept this decision as I began packing. Before placing each item in a box, I wondered if I would ever see it again.

Along with packing, my job also included creating an itemized list to present to the Australian Customs once our container arrived in Brisbane. This was not a problem for a veteran list maker like me. I not only made my list, but I also compiled a 3x5 card with a correlating number for each box. On each card I meticulously wrote every item that was in the box. This technique had been executed in most of our previous moves and had proven to be very helpful when unpacking.

The boxes I had collected for our move began to fill up quickly. Fortunately, our local grocery store agreed to save boxes for us. After making several trips to that store, we finally completed the packing. The hardest part of the move was over for me — until the unpacking would begin once we were in the land down under. My husband and a few of our friends took a day to load the massive container. They packed everything so tightly that nothing would be able to move an inch! I remember the strange feeling I had as I watched that hauler drive away with all of our earthly possessions.

Soon we were boarding our Australia-bound plane. The list for Customs, along with my 3x5 cards, never left my sight. I tucked them along with our passports and other important paper work into my personal carry-on, with a minimal amount of clothes. Each family member followed suit by packing just the essentials. Our container was scheduled to arrive in Brisbane exactly one week after we did. This would give us time to find a place to live.

Once we arrived in Brisbane (Brissy), we quickly found a house to rent. We all were excited to move in and begin to discover Australian living! New beds for each of us, a television to share, and our suitcases were the only furnishings we had. No one really minded "camping" for a few days! It would be an adventure!

Those "few days" turned into weeks with no furniture, and our shipping company had no idea where our container was.

Meanwhile, a kind family we met brought over some basic household items to help us get by. The dishes, silverware, a few pots and pans, folding chairs and some towels they shared with us were greatly appreciated! That first week the kids and I discovered an old table in the bush behind the house. I now understood the adage "Desperate times call for desperate measures" as we cleaned up that table and brought it into the kitchen!

A few times I caught myself sarcastically humming that little tune "If They Could See Me Now" as I thought about my friends and family back in Southern California! This is something they would never do! (Actually, I could hardly believe that I was doing it!)

With no idea where our belongings were, my first and last thought every day was the same: Where was our container and when would it arrive in Brisbane? Daily calls were made to the shipping company, and we received the same answer every time! "We will call you when we know something." It is not a pleasant place to be in, knowing that you can do absolutely nothing to make what you want to happen happen.

Somehow, we had to get on with living. If you have had to do without, or have lost everything you own, you know exactly how we felt. The kids needed to get into a routine of attending their new school, and Len needed to start the process of building our new home. Everyone had something they needed to be doing — except for me. I seemed to be in limbo, and I felt paralyzed. I could feel the huge weight of worry pressing against my chest, and I didn't know how to put it down. Depression began to set in; I was thousands of miles away from anything familiar. How could I be expected to find my routine when I did not have what I needed to make this place our home?

Would we ever see our earthly possessions again? I continued to torture myself by looking at my 3x5 cards. My heart would start to sink, as I hoped our possessions hadn't — photo albums, baby books, my cozy bedspread. I could not leave those cards alone. I knew I should refuse to look at them, but instead they became quite tattered and torn. Most days, sometimes several times a day, I would have to make my way to the back of the house to have a good cry. This became my refuge, a place where no one could see me. Nighttime was even worse. I would lie there, with clenched fists and my stomach in knots, as fear would grip my heart. That container was out there somewhere. I'll bet it did fall into the ocean. (Oh, why didn't we purchase that insurance?) These thoughts continued to plague me night after night.

I seemed to keep praying, the same prayer over and over again: "Lord, let our things get here, so I can get on with making this place home." I realized that these were just possessions, but when you are living in a new place — especially a new country that was so far away — something familiar, anything familiar, would be welcome.

At least six weeks passed before I finally discovered something that I could do: I could make a good decision! This decision proved to be the most powerful thing that I could do.

I gave the whole mess to the Lord. I no longer wanted to carry this worry and concern; it was too heavy for me. I also entertained the thought that, if I never saw our possessions again, I would somehow be OK. I began to thank God each morning for the day; with God's help I would not say, "Maybe today will be the day our container arrives!" Because night was still the most challenging time for me, I would force my hands open, signifying that I was releasing everything. My fears began to dissipate, and my heart felt lighter. I began to realize that I already had what was most important to me: my fam-ily. Fortunately, I had packed my Bible as one of my essentials; peace filled my heart as I read, and God reminded me that I had Him too!

I'd rather not relive that move again.

I am grateful that this experience started the process for me to break free from perfectionism. Living as a perfectionist is like being on a train that runs in circles! You never arrive because there is no destination! Recognizing the destructive effect this cycle has on you is the first counteractive step you can take to break free from perfectionism's deadly grip.

In this chapter ...

... and throughout the book we are going to discover some common triggers ❶ that suck us into trying to or thinking that we need to be perfect. After each trigger we will see some counteractive steps ❷ we can take to disarm the trigger. We will also look at the definition of perfection and perfectionism, and we will see that it is great to want to excel! But first I have to ask ...

Is there really a lighter side?

I can see now that in my former perfectionist years I took the events in my life way too seriously! It's not that life's events don't deserve our attention, they do; but because life is so much better with humor, I am learning to laugh at myself. How about you? Are you able to see the lighter side of unfortunate circumstances? Laughing is a lot better than crying — although sometimes laughter cannot happen until you've had a good cry! (Believe me, there was a lot of crying once we arrived in Australia and our container did not.)

I didn't actually cry the time I forgot the day when the luncheon was at my home, or when I realized I was wearing two different shoes, but I certainly felt a huge lump in my throat. You'll hear more about one of those less-than-perfect experiences in the following chapters, but first I would like you to take a little test, just to see if I'm talking to the right crowd!

Perfectionist Test

Take a minute and answer these questions with either a check mark or a mental yes if this describes you. *Note: These questions were taken from the confessions of real-life perfectionists; the names have been omitted to protect the guilty!*

☐ I can't seem to relax until everything is done.

☐ I procrastinate doing projects I cannot do perfectly.

☐ I have thrown away less than perfect projects so no one will see my mistakes, and I won't be reminded of them.

☐ I feel uncomfortable going out of the house when I don't look my best.

☐ I feel the need to have all of my clothing perfectly matched, and I am intimidated by fashion freedom to wear whatever — just because!

☐ I feel upset if things do not go as planned.

☐ I try to control things.

☐ I clean excessively, even when things don't really need it.

☐ I feel overwhelmed easily when something is out of place.

☐ I have a hard time writing in my journal, or finishing a letter, when I can't find the same color of ink.

☐ I don't let myself forget a mistake I have made, especially if it is a repeated one.

☐ I refold laundry that has been folded by someone else if it is not how I fold it.

☐ I try to maintain control of my emotions at all times.

☐ I have been known to rearrange dirty dishes in the dishwasher.

☐ I place unrealistic demands on others, and I am often disappointed with their work.

☐ I strive to impress others with my abilities and believe they will think less of me if I fail.

Scoring

1 – 2	No worries for you.
3 – 7	You could be headed for trouble.
8 – 11	This book was written for you.
12 – 16	Take a deep breath; you are about to embrace your imperfect life!

Is this really perfectionism?

I hope you survived our little pop quiz! Just for the record, there are a few things that are on that test that aren't necessarily perfectionistic, as long as what is motivating you to do them is beneficial. For instance, most of us will do everything in a particular way, like loading the dishwasher. I load my dishwasher to fit the most in it, and my strategic placement allows me to grab a handful of the same size plates, or type of silverware, etc., when unloading. This helps me complete one of my least favorite tasks in record time!

Now, where I cross the line into perfectionism is when I re-load the entire dishwasher (not just a plate or two) after someone else has loaded it. I cannot accept the way it was done and have to change it. Fortunately, when this happens to me now, I practice being grateful for the help. I also realize that I will have many opportunities to load the dishwasher the way I like it, so I tell myself to chill!

The same goes for folding laundry, and many other tasks we do over and over again. We usually do them in a way that makes sense to us. A side note here: when we solicit or enlist help from family members, we should be willing to accept a less than perfect job! When we don't do that, our helpers will either not be motivated to do a very good job because they know that we will re-do it anyway or they will resent our lack of appreciation for their help. Unfortunately, because of this trait, many perfectionists don't get much help and end up doing whatever it is themselves because it is easier! That is true: a lot of the time it is easier to just do it ourselves; but we miss opportunities to create a desire to work in others, especially our children.

My mom went to work . . .

When I was in 8th grade, my mom went to work, and that meant that I had more responsibility at home. One Christmas she told me I could even decorate the house! (It still amazes me that she would actually let me do that! Now, in my current season of life, I would love it if someone would decorate my house for me!) The amazing thing is, my mom did not change one single thing that I did! We had lived in the same house for many years, so I knew where each decoration was supposed to go, but I am sure that I did not do everything exactly the way she would have done it. I'm pretty sure that I took some decorating liberties by adding my own personal touch!

That Christmas, my mom instilled confidence in me by appreciating and even bragging about my decorating skills. Instilling confidence in others — particularly in children — is a wonderful gift we can give. Unfortunately, we are doing the opposite when we re-do what we have asked them to do or insist that they do everything the way we want it done. Take heart if you have fallen into this pattern; it's never too late to change — and this change will certainly be noticed (and appreciated!) by your kids!

What is perfectionism?

For better understanding, let's take a look at what perfection and perfectionism are, and the difference between the two. We will also look at the definition of a perfectionist and contrast that with what it means to excel.

- The definition of perfection: excellence, worth, goodness, quality and merit
- The definition of perfectionism: refusal to accept any standard short of perfection
- The definition of a perfectionist: one who is fussy, hyper-critical, strict, severe, demanding and fault finding
- The definition of excel: desire to work competently, be skillful, proficient, improve upon or show talent

Notice that the definition of perfection and the definition of excel are similar. The problem occurs when we feel the compulsion to be or do everything perfectly. This makes us into perfectionists, and that leads us to being self-defeating, rigid, unreasonable, driven, and destined to fail.

While healthy achievers (those who desire to excel) usually find great pleasure in a job well done, they are also able to keep a rational perspective. They realize that some tasks have no room for error, such as piloting a plane or performing brain surgery, while other jobs, like preparing for a meeting, leading a group, planning a vacation, or even writing a book, can be far less exacting! While the healthy achiever finds satisfaction, the perfectionist finds pain.

When you take an honest look at perfectionism, you will see that it really is an illusion. To gain some clarity, here are some synonyms for illusion: fallacy, false impression, head trip, false appearance and false belief. No one is interested in investing time and energy in something that is not real or is impossible to achieve.

None of us are perfect, nor will we ever become perfect; and the harder we try to be, the more discouraged we become. Perfectionism is a compelling force that causes us to think that we need to be more that we are capable of being. This driving force causes us to always be striving and rarely allows us to enjoy our achievements.

We cannot enjoy them because, for one, we don't think the job was that well done. For another, we have set the bar too high, and in so doing we have backed ourselves into a corner of trying to outdo ourselves or others. We fear to fail, and those fears become magnified. To deviate from our inner illusions of perfection in any way would mean — would mean what? It would mean that we are fallible, vulnerable, human and normal — just like everybody else. This is a huge hurdle for the perfectionist to get over, but this realization brings liberty!

Do I have to lower my standards?

I want to make it clear here: breaking free from the grip of perfectionism does not mean lowering your standards or changing how you prefer to do things. But it does mean acknowledging and accepting that sometimes things turn out great, and sometimes they don't; and that is OK! I have found this quite rewarding. I make myself see that perfection is not the goal, getting the job done is!

Discovering the why . . .

Why do we get caught in this trap called perfectionism so easily? How did you get caught? Perhaps it has been modeled for you. Or maybe the constant chaos you grew up with has made you not want to be like that — even a little bit. Perfectionism blurs the fine line between doing our best and being obsessed by it!

Common Triggers

Before I tell you the rest of the story about our move to Australia, I'd like to direct you to some common triggers that turn on our perfectionist impulses; most of us don't even realize it when we yield to them. We certainly don't realize the extent of the destruction they cause. If we did, we would do whatever we needed to do to stop it!

🅣 Control and Manipulation

It's true! You and I have so little control over circumstances, like what I experienced in our move to Australia. It is also a waste of both time and energy when we try to control or manipulate them. Looking back, I can see that I was trying to make the shipping company feel responsible and sorry about our lost container by calling them — every single day. This really was a waste of my time, and it put me in a foul mood for the rest of the day. A weekly call would have been sufficient, but that would have taken more self-control than I had!

You run into a lot of frustration when you are a control freak and can't control every aspect of your life! Often times we do this without even realizing it!

🅒 Counteraction: Mind your own business!

Understanding and accepting your inability to control circumstances or other people will bring great benefit to you — and to those people you are trying to control too! "Mind your own business!" Easy to say but hard to do! Staying out of other people's business is a great benefit to them and fosters healthy relationships. It takes wisdom, practice, and self-control to know when to be quietly supportive and to not take the reins out of someone else's hands.

🅒 Counteraction: Define what you are responsible for.

Being responsible for yourself is a much lighter task than taking on the responsibility for the world — or your world, to be more specific! There is great value in understanding that you really can't control what other people do or do not do. Define what your responsibility is in the situation. This is one of the first steps to steering yourself away from being controlling and manipulative.

Here is some good news!

There is something that you actually can control. You and I can take control of how we choose to respond to someone or to a situation. Although this is not easy, nor is it for wimps, it can be very empowering!

It was through the challenges I faced during our long-distance move that something very significant began to happen in my life. I could sense it — but at the time I did not know that this experience would be the beginning of the process for me to break away from perfectionism. My inability to control this situation made me realize for the first time that I could only control my response to it.

I also learned that trading my anxiety for God's peace was a good trade! My attitude about our possessions began to change too. Because of this experience, my possessions no longer have a hold on me. I was learning to hold them, and to hold them with an open hand.

Control and manipulation are fear based.

Just like living a perfect life is impossible to achieve, so is trying to control circumstances and people. Always trying to take control can easily become an addiction, and that addiction is motivated by fear. This compulsive behavior will set in you a destructive pattern that will whittle away at how you value yourself as a person and will lower your self-confidence.

The problem is that we think we are in control, and we think we are being the strong ones when we try to manipulate people and situations. We try to get people to do what we want them to do because we are convinced that we know what the right thing to do is — and we are fearful that they don't!

Sometimes our manipulation is successful, if the people we are trying to control can easily be swayed or bullied or shamed into action. The need to control or to manipulate is a sign of weakness on our part. Likewise choosing to only take responsibility for ourselves is a sign of confidence! Because this is necessary in every relationship and in every situation, we will have a lot of opportunities to get really good at this! Practice makes perfect! (Tell me that I did not just say that — I think you know what I mean!)

🅣 False humility and justification

These next two triggers go hand in hand: when we either try to conceal or downplay the perfectionist impulses or to explain ourselves all the time. I have done both, but trying to conceal or play it down was more my norm. People seemed to consistently comment on my organization abilities or how everything I did was so perfect — which made me want to crawl in a hole and hide! I was not trying to draw attention to what I was doing, so why were they watching my every move? Or were they? No, actually they weren't; I just thought they were.

I was becoming self-conscious; I allowed their comments to make me feel the need to act as if I didn't want everything to be perfect, when I actually did. So I would use false humility by pointing out less than perfect areas in my life. I wanted to feel accepted instead of isolated.

🅒 Counteraction

My counteractive step to false humility is short and sweet, but not always an easy thing to do. When someone comments on how I do this or that, I try very hard to just say thank you — and leave it at that! Another thing I could do: allow others see my not so perfect self. This was not easy either, but when I started doing it, I realized that it felt good!

🅣 Justification

When I tried to justify my perfectionism, my response would be, "I guess I'm just a perfectionist." It took me a while to learn the difference between trying to be perfect and doing a good job.

I thought it was necessary to explain my life away! As long as I knew why I was doing something, that was good enough — and for the most part I did!

🅒 Counteraction: Drop your defense!

Another counteraction — and an important part of my healing process — was allowing myself to be perfectly fine with a dinner that was not very good! Now, instead of making excuses or acting defensively, I try to learn from my mistakes and make improvements. And sometimes the best action is to throw the recipe away — and don't forget to laugh!

● Counteraction: Give yourself some grace.

I practice forgiving myself when I forget to do something for someone that I said I would do — even if that someone is not willing to forgive me! (I still go to a class, even when I have not done my homework too!) These kinds of things happen, not all of the time — thank goodness — but they do happen. And they are a normal part of life.

When we yield to either of these triggers, false humility or justification, we are not living and enjoying life like we could. Ponder what counteractions resonate with you, and get ready to use them to disarm these triggers when they come - because they will certainly come! When you fail (I did say "when" not "if") and allow yourself to be sucked back into any of these triggers, realize it with acknowledgment, and don't beat yourself up over it! Apply a counteractive step ASAP, and remember that developing new habits take time. You will get this!

The lost has been found!

Before you finish this chapter, as promised, I want to share with you the "rest of the story." The lost was found; our container had not fallen into the ocean! Instead of in Brisbane, it arrived in Hong Kong, and it was sitting in the shipping yard there. Once it had been identified as ours, it was loaded on the next ship headed for Brisbane.

However, there were more delays. Our container was held in quarantine for an additional week. Remember the boxes that I got from the grocery store? They were apple boxes. Fruit boxes don't make it through customs (remember that if you ever move to another country!). They had to be burned to ensure there would be no danger of contamination to Australian fruit. Everything in those boxes needed to be repacked in safe boxes.

I would like to be able to tell you that this news did not rattle me, but it did. I felt responsible for this delay and the extra charges for new boxes and for repacking them. But I was the only one thinking about that. The excitement of my family was contagious, and eventually my focus shifted from regret to thankfulness. I was thankful that our stuff was not somewhere on the bottom of the ocean and had finally arrived in Brisbane!

The first time I spoke publicly about this experience, in jest, I called it the perfect move! It took two containers to deliver our belongings to us. Apparently, whoever repacked our things could not get as much in a box as I could. Or perhaps because they would charge us for the boxes, they used them liberally! Nevertheless, it's too bad they did not have my index cards, so they could have gotten it right!

After the initial shock over how quickly they must have re-packed our items wore off, I began to find it quite amusing as I unpacked. I found shoes and pots and pans in the same box; I even found a box of towels that had one shoe in it! I certainly did not need those tattered index cards; they were no help at all! It took a very long time to sort things out and find a place for everything, but we did. Our new abode was shaping up nicely and starting to feel like home — although I was amazed that, even after drastically paring down before our long distance move, we still had too much stuff! I think I realized this because we had learned to live with less for the last six weeks. By Australian standards we must have looked like hoarders!

In this chapter . . .

We saw the difference between perfect and perfectionism, and we saw that desiring excellence is a good thing — but not always possible. We also realized that giving our best is enough - and when we believe that, we re-move the pressure to perform. We were encouraged to be on the look-out for the triggers of false humility & justification and of control & manipulation, and to become familiar with the counteractions we can take to keep those triggers at bay!

In the next chapter . . .

We will look at several more triggers that try to pull us into perfectionism like a magnet and counteractive steps we can take to break that connection!

I will also tell you how an accident sealed the deal for me in wanting to kiss perfectionism good-bye! I can't wait to share with you the life changing principles I learned, because you can learn them too – without the accident!

CHAPTER 2

There's a crack in everything. That's how the light gets in.

~ Leonard Cohen

Enjoying Our Imperfect Lives

We can make our plans . . .

While in the emergency room, I tried to convince myself that we would still be able to make our trip the next day. Thinking clearly was difficult for me because of the pain I was experiencing; I hoped the medication would kick in soon.

The day had started out with a list of things to do before we traveled to see Len's brother in Dallas. My daughter had been helping me wash all of the windows in our home, inside and out. I decided I could take care of the last few windows myself. I did not make it very far up the ladder before it began to slide down the side of the house, with me still on it! As the extension ladder came crashing to the ground, my right foot got caught under the rung.

Have you ever wished that you would wake up and discover that what you had just experienced was only a bad dream? That's what I wished for, every morning that first week after my fall. Unfortunately as I woke and my eyes began to focus, the wheel chair beside my bed was the first thing I saw. Realization began to set in that this was my new reality.

I had crushed my heel, shattering it into several pieces. Placing three pins and a bone graft into my heel was the plan; I hoped and prayed for a successful surgery. My surgeon was one of the best, but he was noncommittal about my recovery and ability to walk again without pain. His instructions to me were to follow the exercise plan I was given and keep weight off my foot for at least three months. It sounded bleak to me that the range of motion that I would have at the one-year mark would be what I would have for the rest of my life.

We can make our plans, but needless to say we never made our trip to Dallas, and I suddenly had a lot of time on my hands. Isn't it interesting how many days (and weeks for that matter) we spend wondering how in the world we are ever going to get everything done that we need to? And isn't it just as amazing how we make our plans, but it only takes one event to bring everything to a screeching halt? Perhaps you can relate?

It's hard to put your life on hold.

My mind raced with worry about how I would cover my responsibilities and what everyday life was going to be like now. After a few days passed, I remembered a favorite Bible verse, "And we know that God causes everything to work together for the good of those who love God and are called according to His purpose." I held on to that promise, and through tears I asked the Lord to help me learn everything I needed to get through this experience. Little did I know my life was about to change forever!

They started coming . . .

Friends and family started to come to see me. They brought wonderful things with them, like flowers, books, cards, goodies, dinners — and even offered to clean my home! As they came, I felt the Lord whisper that His plan for me was to receive anything and everything they wanted to give me, and to receive it with a thankful heart. The Lord was giving me permission to enjoy others serving me. I wanted to say "You should not have done that!" or "No, we don't need anything. We are just fine." Instead, I had to bite my tongue and say thank you. Not only did I need to learn how to receive, but I needed to learn how to receive joyfully.

Why is receiving so hard?

Looking back on that time, I remember being truly amazed by the kindness of family and friends, by seeing how much I was loved. And I was in no position to reciprocate. Not only is it "more blessed to give that it is to receive" but it's a whole lot easier too! Why is it so hard to receive? Perhaps it is so hard because it humbles us when we realize that we need help.

We take turns!

Another whisper I heard from the Lord, "You are reaping what you have sown." I have enjoyed many opportunities to send a card, give a gift, or prepare a meal for someone in need. Was this what God was trying to tell me? Receiving became a bit little easier when I realized that we take turns being the needy one.

One of my greatest blessings, as well as one of my greatest challenges, was learning to receive from my husband, Len. I used to pride myself on being the one who served him, and I rarely asked for his help. Boy, was that about to change! I was so needy; and fortunately for me, he was willing to give. He even served me cheerfully! He really had meant it when he said, "For better or for worse!"

I grew up believing happily-ever-after was actually possible. My parents were older when they had me, and they didn't argue. I guess they got that over with during their early years of marriage! They also took difficulties in their stride — again a sign of maturity. I needed to learn for myself that being joyful or peaceful was not determined by my circumstances. My plans were not the only thing that came to a screeching halt when disaster struck, so did my joy!

I am not saying that we need to dance for joy when something bad happens, but having peace in our hearts certainly helps us to gain God's perspective! In my striving for perfection, even a regular bump in the road would send me into a tail spin. It took this irregular bump in my road for me to learn some principles that would change my life forever!

In this chapter . . .

I will share those principles with you. We will also look at more triggers, like performance-based love, being a people pleaser, playing the blame game (both versions), and having unrealistic expectations, and at the counteractions we can take that will move us from striving for perfection to thriving in our imperfect lives!

Principles I learned

With all of this time on my hands, I had some pondering to do . . .

As I elaborate on these thoughts, perhaps you may wish to consider them too.

Just say thank you . . .

Why is it so hard to say thank you? When someone compliments me on how I look, I often respond by saying, "I need a haircut," or "I've had this old shirt for ages!" When someone commends me on a job well done, I am quick to give the credit to those who helped me. It is good to recognize team work, but I quickly gave a pass to any recognition for my part of the job.

Even when people were impressed with my decorating skills, I'd try to draw their attention to all of the things that I still needed to do. Instead, I could have said — and this is really quite simple — "THANK YOU"! Here's an assignment: practice saying "thank you" anytime someone says something nice to you! For extra credit, stop right after you say thank you, and don't say another word!

When there is no visible sign of appreciation from the recipient, I can feel a little deflated. Before my accident, it never occurred to me that they might not know what to say. Or that they might have felt embarrassed or awkward being recipients. Now I can relate to each of these. Even my sometimes fumbled but always heartfelt thank-you was a gift I could give to those who showed kindness to me.

Perhaps I took this license to receive a little too far; after several weeks of practicing this principle, I began to feel a little like a kid at Christmas when dinner was at the door!

Life needs to be simplified . . .

I want to warn you that these next two thoughts I had to ponder are personal. After you read them, I might lose my credibility as a prudent person! When on crutches and even using my wheel chair, going to the bathroom held several challenges for me. First of all, it took me a lot longer to get there. Once I arrived, I still needed to get into the door; this was especially challenging in public restrooms. Many of the handicapped stalls were not easy to maneuver around in, especially in a wheel chair - weren't they designed for that?!? I then had to back up, line myself up with the toilet, and pull my shorts and underwear down quickly, all while hopping and balancing on one foot!

The thought of additional surgery if I placed any weight on my foot was enough to keep me hopping, when it was absolutely necessary. I needed some simplification here! At least it was summer, and I could wear loose shorts and not jeans. I never would have thought that (temporarily) not wearing underwear would simplify my life in such a helpful way, but it did!

What used to be important wasn't even necessary . . .

Lining the toilet seat in a public restroom – not gonna happen! For the first time in my life, my backside got used to landing on an unprepared toilet seat! Although this was not my preferred method, I am living proof that it can be done without contracting unthinkable diseases! Please don't tell my mom!

We really don't know how people feel until we experience similar suffering . . .

One really good thing that can come from any kind of suffering is developing empathy. I knew firsthand how much it meant when people went out of their way to talk to me about my injury, especially when they had experienced a similar one. Many of them didn't even know me. I hung on their every word, especially when some told me that they had a full recovery and full range of motion!

My heart still hurts when I see someone with a foot injury. I try to encourage each of them just like I have been encouraged. Yes, my life was about to change. God was going to free me from the bondage of perfectionism one step at a time — even though I could not walk!

Let's look at the triggers in this chapter that lead us into perfectionism.

Performance-based love

Performance-based love was at the root of my perfectionism. Even though I never got a confession out of her (when I was growing up, parents didn't talk about such things), I'm pretty sure my mom thought she was going through menopause instead of being pregnant with me! I can imagine the surprise when they discovered that I was on my way to join the family.

Although there was a significant age difference between me and my siblings, they too seemed to enjoy having a little sister — most of the time anyway. From the time I was a small child, I fulfilled the role of the entertainer. The spotlight seemed to always be on me to do something photo worthy or to make my family laugh. This is quite common, especially for the baby of the family.

I knew my parents loved me (they had to — I was their kid!), but unfortunately this generation of parents didn't say "I love you" or offer verbal affirmation very often. This is why I grew up thinking that people would only love and accept me for what I could do for them or bring to the table. I felt the need to always prove my worth. And this is one of the ways I yielded to the trigger of performance-based love.

Unfortunately, I didn't know how to put this burden down because, most of the time, I didn't even realize that I was carrying it. As you adjust to carrying weight, your mind will also adjust. Similar to when you carry a back pack, after a while you hardly notice the effort you are exerting in carrying it until you take it off.

Now that I have laid the weight of performance-based love down, I realize just how heavy it was! And because I never want to pick that weight up again, I need to watch for signs of this destructive trigger.

Looking at the opposite behavior to these triggers is helpful in discovering the counteractions we can take. And take them we must, for if we do not, we will be yielding to the damaging nature of the trigger. The trigger will not only lead us into perfectionism but will keep us there!

ⓒ Counteraction: Ask for h e l p!

One counteraction to performance-based love you can take is accepting help from others. That was a little easier for me when I crushed my heel because I really didn't have a choice. Before my accident I used to take pride in thinking that I did not need any help! I would struggle through something when it would have been much better (and usually faster) to have help. Sometimes I would refuse help and then complain about my lack of help — oh dear!

This is still a challenge for me, but I am trying to develop a habit of asking for help when I need it!

ⓒ Counteraction: Just say no.

Learning to say no is another way you can stop performance-based love dead in its tracks! This is a little easier to do when you do not give your answer right away. Make it clear that you would like to think or pray about what is being asked of you first. Developing this pattern of response gives you time to make a wise decision. When I really am not sure, I ask someone who knows me and my schedule for input.

Sometimes I end up saying no and then realize that I really would like to do whatever was asked of me. I find it much easier to go back and say yes than to have to change my initial yes to a no — those are never fun conversations to have!

ⓣ People pleaser

Being a people pleaser goes hand in hand with performance-based love, and they both are a hard way to live! One of the problems with being a people pleaser is that people are not always pleased! Demanding people are rarely pleased with any effort, and they always expect more.

It's interesting that, with all the admiration for the overachiever in our society, there is also admiration for the person who does not live life by pleasing others. I don't mean that such people are not considerate or kind, but they are confident enough to stand their ground (in things that matter) in an admirable way! I'd rather be that kind of person instead of always saying yes to everyone!

© Counteraction: Be true to you!

By being true to yourself, you embrace who you are and — just as important - who you are not!

Being true to you is not as easy as it sounds. It takes courage to change your ways, and some people may be upset with you when you do. But change you must if you are going to really enjoy your life and live free from perfectionism.

There is freedom to be enjoyed when you no longer allow yourself to be pressured into saying yes or feel like you will no longer be loved (or loved as much) if you do not do what is being asked of you. An interesting repercussion of exercising this freedom: others will eventually respect you for it!

❶ Blame

The blame game not only creates a vicious cycle but is another trigger for perfectionism. It is not easy to admit when you've messed up - I still find this challenging! Pride is the core issue here when we try to shift the blame either to someone else or to the circumstances. The blame game redirects the focus off our weakness and onto to someone else's. It's hard enough for us to accept our own imperfection; we don't want anyone else to see it either!

Defensiveness

Blaming others brings along with it a defensiveness which alienates you from cultivating healthy relationships. Do you find it as hard as I do to say "I was wrong"? Perhaps you could practice forming those words — when no one is around, of course! Not everyone is going to shout with glee when you own up to a mistake you have made — and that's OK. Give people time and space to come around; but if they never do, you are still better for your decision to not blame others.

Don't volunteer to be the fall guy or gal!

Some of us can fall into the habit of taking the blame for others' mistakes. When you become the fall guy for someone else, you're taking responsibility for something that you cannot make right. You're also enabling that person's irresponsible behavior, which is destructive for everyone!

One exception

We do need to acknowledge responsibility for a child or someone in our care. And in those situations the offender needs to take responsibility too, so he or she can grow through the experience. We have all been around people (or perhaps have even been this type of person) who are defensive and want to believe that their child can do no wrong! It is humbling when our child causes harm to someone or something. In fighting perfectionism, it is imperative that we accept that our kids are going to do this at some point. We also need to have a plan of action for when that happens. We will talk more about families and our imperfect relationships in Chapter Five.

What if it's not your fault?

It is especially challenging not to blame others for your misfortune when they are the cause of it! It's hard enough when you have to suffer from your own actions, but suffering from the actions of someone else — don't you have a right to complain?

There is benefit in voicing how you feel — to a trusted source. In doing this you are being true to yourself and acknowledging the gamut of emotions you are feeling.

Ⓒ Counteraction: Process through why you blame.

I want to offer caution here: there is no benefit to making yourself at home in the camp of the offended. When you're stuck blaming, you will be controlled by it, and your perceptions will be skewed by the dark cloud cast on everything you do. As the offended, you become the prisoner, confined by the actions of the offender. Haven't you given your offender enough power already? Instead, keep moving by committing yourself to process through your experience.

The definition of process is: developing a series of steps that you can take in order to achieve a particular end.

A great first step for me is becoming aware of what circumstances propel me to blame others, for instance, when I have not given myself enough time to do something. Now, instead of casting blame elsewhere, I try to realize my error in timing, and I attempt to learn from it!

Another step is to seek to understand why I turn to blame. I tend to shift the blame elsewhere when I am disappointed in myself.

Ⓒ Counteraction (this one brings true freedom): Forgive.

I can't explain how it happens, but when we are able to forgive (and it takes time), we are released from being held hostage by those who have hurt us. Forgiveness is not giving the offender a pass but releasing her or him from blame.

Forgiveness is necessary, but rarely is it easy. I have personally found that forgiving is not impossible — even when I was convinced that it was going to be! I have also found that it is the best way to live — free and in peace!

Jesus tells us that if we want to be forgiven, we must forgive others. We all need forgiveness, and when we realize that, it places forgiving others in the proper perspective.

I think it is a good idea to sow seeds of forgiveness liberally to everyone! There is a good chance that we will need to be forgiven a time or two.

Ⓒ Counteraction: Embrace humility.

Believe me, it takes humility to honestly admit when we are wrong or have made a mess of things! Yet, when we take responsibility for our actions with humility, we acknowledge ourselves as imperfect beings and forgive ourselves for having messed up.

Facing the consequences of our actions is not pleasant, but that too has its rewards. Telling the truth by admitting that we are at fault lightens our heart and will set us free! When we choose to tell the truth, we will experience what John 8:32 promises: and the truth will set you free.

ⓣ Shame

There is another version of the blame-game. Let's call it the shame-game. This version comes into play when blame turns to shame, because we are blaming and shaming ourselves.

Shame is allowing something that we have done to transfer into who we now think that we are.

Let me explain. In my former perfectionist years, whenever I made a mistake, I would allow myself to feel shamed, and this began to cloud my perception and my identity. Even after I apologized for my behavior (when necessary), I could not seem to forgive myself. I would replay my part in the painful situation over and over, believing that everything was my fault. I chided myself, treating myself most unfairly, which in turn chiseled away at my self-esteem . . . Can you see my downward slide?

The truth is: we all will make mistakes and poor choices sometimes, but they do not define who we are! Aren't you glad that none of us are powerful enough to have everything . . . be . . . our . . . fault?!?

We're not quite done with shame . . .

There is another side to shame: when we seek to bring shame on another. I heard "shame on you" more than once while growing up, and it never moved me in a positive or productive direction. Instead, it made me feel stuck right there in my shame.

It is good to remember how it feels to be shamed, because that will help us not want to inflict that pain on anyone else. Some of the most grace-filled, forgiving people I know are the ones who have experienced a great deal of forgiveness themselves! They don't shame, and they don't blame; they seem to know when you just need a big hug!

ⓒ Counteraction: Don't be afraid to be vulnerable

Present yourself as vulnerable. When you do, you will live shame free! As an added benefit, when you present yourself as vulnerable and choose to be transparent, you encourage others to do likewise.

I have the opportunity to practice being transparent in a vulnerable way when I teach a *Your Home Matters* class. *Your Home Matters*, my first book, is about enjoying your home while lowering your stress through effective home management and de-cluttering. The course has grown out of that book. Although as the teacher I am considered the expert, when I shift my focus from trying to dazzle others with my expertise, achievements, and attempts to always be right (which spells PERFECTIONISM in all caps!) to connecting with people through my vulnerability, I have their attention!

Being transparent has reduced my stress level in measurable ways because it leaves room for error. The only thing that I want to prove to my students is the fact that none of us, and none of our homes, are perfect — and that it is possible to enjoy them anyway! You will hear more about our homes in Chapter Four.

🛈 Unrealistic expectations

There are realistic expectations in any relationship, like faithfulness, truthfulness, courtesy, and kindness. (Actually, there are more, but you get the idea.) It is when our expectations cross the line and become unrealistic — like not being disappointed, never needing to compromise, or thinking that other people are supposed to make us happy, to mention just a few — that we make ourselves miserable!

Here are some personal, painful examples – that, thank goodness, I can laugh at now!

Opposites attract

In a marriage, these opposing traits can quickly lead to disaster when either spouse unrealistically expects to be able to change her or his mate!

Let me give you a personal example. My family was never late to anything; if anything, they leaned way the other way. For instance, if you went shopping with my mom, you were guaranteed to spend time waiting in the car until the store opened. I come from a long line of these types of people. Both her mother (my grandmother) and her two sisters were exactly the same way.

I'm not sure how my husband, Len, was raised, but I do know that he never wants to arrive early to anything! Many times we would arrive late to events, which did not make me very happy. It was not what I wanted, and it was not what I expected, but it was my new reality. My disapproval of our lack of punctuality would put a wedge between us on the way to wherever we were going. This created an additional problem for me, for, as a perfectionist, I did not want other people to know we were mad at each other — you know, the perfect marriage! So I would try to quickly patch things up, sometimes as we were walking up to the door wherever we were going! He would not have it! My hubby was not bothered by being late; he also was not bothered as much as I was when we weren't getting along.

Along with being the time keeper, I also assigned myself the job of gas tank monitor. I consistently pointed out to Len when the gas tank was getting low (in my family being low on fuel meant you still had a quarter of a tank left), and I had the unreasonable expectation that he would think the same way! The more I nagged him, the more he dug in his heels — and would trust in fumes alone!

I was trying to control our being on time; what our friends, family, or acquaintances thought about us once we arrived; and having enough gas to actually get there! All of these expectations I was placing on Len were unrealistic. I was used to seeing my mom get her own way with my dad most of the time, but Len would not be controlled. Let's just say that the sparks that flew early in our marriage were not all fireworks!

Now if we are late, I realize that it is not the end of the world! If I'm feeling anxious, I try to think that perhaps we have missed a terrible accident on the freeway, etc., so I try to chill (deep breathing helps too). And the probability of us really running out of gas is slim: my hubby has coasted into more gas stations than could be counted, so the odds are in our favor! Besides, it is really not my problem to solve, unless I am the one driving. And if we do run out of gas, this too is not the end of the world. I then would have time to catch up on my reading — thankful I can read my books on my phone, anywhere, anytime!

Progress has been made!

I am relieved to tell you that we have worked these things out. We are rarely late. (Come to find out Len did not like arriving late either; he just didn't appreciate being nagged about it.) We usually arrive at our destination speaking to each other; and if we run out of gas, we run out of gas. Most of the time I can keep my mouth shut, unless I think Len is not aware of the condition of the gas tank. During those times, he has been grateful for my attentiveness — imagine that!

Ⓒ Counteraction: Temper all expectations with reality.

Here is another personal example: When I ask Len if he will take out the trash, I must realize that he might not do it at the very minute I ask him to, or he might forget. (He has his reasons for not jumping when I ask; I think he might be trying to help me with the controlling trigger!) Anyway, back to the trash: If I need it taken out immediately, I take it out! If not, he can do it when he is ready; and if he forgets, I try to not make a big deal out of it!

Does anyone really have a perfect life?

We all know the answer to that, but it's easy for us perfectionists to think there is something wrong with our lives when things go wrong. (I'll bet you have had days like my messy day I told you about at the beginning of this book.) After the first mishap, we start checking off one annoying situation after another, and, without realizing it, we're expecting more to come, taking the joy right out of the day.

Why do we think that our day — or, even more so, our life — needs to run smoothly to be a good one? Buying into the Why me syndrome is never a good purchase! Do we ever consider Why not me? Is there any reason that I should never have a flat tire, have someone cut me off on the freeway, or even get into an accident? Is there any reason that I should never get sick or experience loss? These types of things happen all of the time, and, some days, the best part of the day is when it is finally over! I have known people who never seem to hit any bumps at all — or so I thought. I was wrong; they hit bumps just like me. The difference was that they do something most of us don't do: they change their attitudes toward the bumps!

In this chapter . . .

I truly hope that you can adopt the principles that I learned during the aftermath of my accident. I also hope that you will join me in stepping down from the platform of performance-based love, stepping back from people pleasing, and stepping away from playing the blame game, either version. One last thing: if you keep these in mind and your expectations are realistic, you will send your perfectionism packing!

In the next chapter . . .

I will break some unbelievable news for you about Barbie and super models. We will uncover more triggers (some of my most challenging ones) to keep our perfectionist ways at bay. So, if you are ready to ditch the notion of being and doing everything perfectly, and, more importantly, if you are ready to fully embrace and enjoy how you are put together, you're going to like this next chapter!

CHAPTER 3

Once you accept the fact that you're not perfect,
then you develop some confidence.

~ *Rosalynn Carter*

Enjoying Our Beautiful Imperfect Selves

Several years ago I attended a women's conference at Camp Crestview in Corbett, Oregon. It was exciting for me because I had attended this camp as a teenager. After preparing to leave for the weekend and several hours of driving, my excitement waned; all of my traveling buddies were tired too. I'm sure that contributed to the uneasy feeling I had as I entered the auditorium for the evening session. As I inspected the cuteness of the worship team, I wished I had changed from my wrinkled traveling clothes. Self-consciously I tried to conceal my hands - what I wanted to do was sit on them! I hoped no one would notice my chipped fingernail polish.

The lights dimmed, and the team left the stage as the Rocky theme began to play and strobe lights came on. The change in atmosphere took my attention away from what I was wearing and my neglected nails. All eyes began to focus on someone who appeared to be moving in slow motion down the center aisle. As she reached the stage, her appearance became clearer. She was breathing hard, dressed in her gray sweats that had lumps and bumps in the problem areas of a woman's anatomy! Through gestures and dialog, she quickly drew us into her thoughts and struggles about the exercise class she portrayed she was attending.

You could have heard a pin drop as the packed auditorium watched her every move. The Rocky theme faded and the music shifted to an aerobic beat. She was new to this class, she related to us, and, feeling self-conscious, she quickly made her way to the back of the room. Her wobbly legs almost failed her as she tripped over the edge of an exercise mat belonging to an extremely fit girl in pink. She tried not to stare, but that was hard when she realized that her sweat band could fit around pinky's waistline!

Once her safe spot was secured and class started, she let out a gasp. She spotted someone in the room who looked worse than she did! She too was struggling with the routine! Hmm, she was beginning to feel a little better. Perhaps this class her friend had convinced her to take (Where was she anyway?) was not going to be that bad! Again, trying not to stare, she still managed to keep one eye on that poor struggling lady as the class progressed.

"Time for cool down," the instructor shouted as the music took on a slower pace. Yes, she had somehow made it through the class! She quickly gathered up her mat. She wanted to speak to that struggling woman — as soon as she could catch her breath. Perhaps she could make a new friend! She looked around but she couldn't find the woman - How had she gotten out of there so fast?

Just then everything changed! She needed to get out of there — and fast too! She doubted she could ever return! You see, there had never been another woman: all along she had been seeing her own reflection in the mirrors along the back wall!

Again you could have heard a pin drop in the auditorium. Once we had a minute to process all that had been related to us, wild cheering broke out. Soon we were all on our feet offering this awesome woman a standing ovation! Whoever wrote that skit got it, totally understanding just how hard it can be trying to feel like you fit in. Because it took several minutes for the crowd to settle down, I knew I was not the only one who could relate.

I no longer cared that I had not changed my clothes as I grabbed my notebook; holding my pen, I was no longer concerned about my chipped fingernails either. I knew that this was going to be a great conference!

Common Ground

That skit set the tone and contributed to the success of the conference. It pointed out common ground that helped the audience connect. Instead of feeling self-conscious, I no longer felt like I had to compete with the other women in the room; I felt like their equal - we were all in this together! It did this perfectionist good to realize that we all share similar insecurities. The need to be dressed or act in a certain way can easily become an obsession, and truly spells insecurity! I am the first to admit that I still prefer to be dressed similar to those I will be with, but I am certainly thankful that I don't obsess over it like I used to.

In this chapter . . .

Unfortunately, negative self-talk, comparing ourselves to others, and feeling the need to impress will shatter our confidence and sabotage amazing opportunities. Each of these triggers will drag us onto the path of perfectionism. We will talk about each one of them in this chapter, as well as some counteractions that will keep the beast of perfectionism at bay.

Barbie, we're not through with you!

Several years ago I listened to an unbelievable talk-show interview with a woman who had taken the Barbie image too far. At the hand of a plastic surgeon, she had been made to look just like Barbie. She had spent every penny of her one-hundred-thousand-dollar inheritance on this transformation. Equally amazing, I later learned from a follow-up story I read, a man watching the same talk show decided he wanted some surgery too. After spending a fortune himself, he began to resemble the Ken doll. He even changed his name to Miles Kendall because he looked miles better and enjoyed looking like the Ken doll (his words)! These are extreme measures!

Lasting perfection is not possible, even for Barbie!

After time, even perfect Barbie begins to show some wear and tear, with hair starting to resemble a haystack (especially after some of us cut off her cute pony tail); even her stylish, blue eyeshadow fades with time!

I hope you enjoy this little tidbit (by an unknown author that I found in several places on the Internet and have modified). Finally, a Barbie we can relate to!

Soccer Mom Barbie - All that experience as a cheer-leader is really paying off as Barbie dusts off her old, high school megaphone to cheer for Babs and Ken Jr. She comes with minivan and cooler filled with bagged snacks and juice boxes.

Flabby Arms Barbie - Hide Barbie's droopy triceps with these new, roomier-sleeved gowns; tummy-support panels are included.

Bunion Barbie - Years of disco dancing in stiletto heels have definitely taken their toll on Barbie's dainty arched feet. Soothe her feet with the pumice stone, foot soaking tub, and soft terry slippers.

No-More-Wrinkles Barbie - Erase those pesky crow's-feet and lip lines with a tube of Skin Sparkle-Spackle, from Barbie's own line of exclusive age-blasting cosmetics.

Bifocal Barbie - Comes with her own set of fashion frames in six wild colors (half-frames too!); neck chain and large-print editions of Vogue are included.

Recovery Barbie - Too many parties have finally caught up with the ultimate party girl. Now she does the Twelve Steps instead of the two-step. Clean and sober, she's going to meetings religiously. She comes with a little copy of The Big Book and a six-pack of Diet Coke.

Hot Flash Barbie - Press Barbie's bellybutton and watch her face turn beet red while tiny drops of perspiration appear on her forehead. Comes with battery operated fan and tiny tissues.

Facial Hair Barbie - As Barbie's hormone levels shift, see her whiskers grow; available with tiny tweezers and 10x magnifying mirror.

Post-Menopausal Barbie - This Barbie wets her pants when she sneezes, forgets where she puts things, and cries a lot. Comes with Depends and Kleenex. As a bonus, the book Life After Menopause is included.

Continuing with fiction for a moment

If you were given three wishes from your (ahem) fairy godmother, would any of your wishes be to change something in your physical appearance? A million dollars would undeniably be tempting, but I sure could think of some physical changes I'd ask for instead!

Unfortunately, very few of us feel comfortable with the way we look. Although we can boost our confidence by trying to look our best using what is available to us, most procedures are temporary or could lead to another . . . and another, like the woman who underwent operation after operation to look like Barbie!

Super Models - not so super

All it took was being in one fashion show as a girl to start my daydreaming about becoming a model. I really liked Twiggy: she was cute; she was young; she was from London; and she was flat-chested! What a great job — the beautiful clothes, wonderful places to travel to, and the riches!

Yes, some models are paid a lot of money, but there is no way that this is an easy job! Can you imagine being under the watchful eye of the world? You have probably seen a clip of one of those beautiful models trying to regain her composure after tripping or stumbling down — or even off — the runway. Can you imagine how you might feel knowing that you are entertaining the masses as they watch and share those YouTube videos?

There is not much job security either. This world is fickle; you could be a top model today but not tomorrow. How about the self-control needed in both eating and exercise? Let's just say that most of us have no idea! And, as if that isn't hard enough, sometimes this rigid self-control turns into a relentless eating or exercise disorder.

Nor is there any privacy either. The more famous the model is, the less privacy she has; someone will always be trying to make a buck at her expense! Being a super model is not so super!

I have to confess!

I enjoy seeing photos of super models or stars without any make-up — especially the ones in which you can hardly recognize them! I think I enjoy seeing them because I am reminded that they are just people! I'll bet they enjoy those times too, when they can take a break from the pressures of being stars — until someone plasters their photos on the front page of a tabloid! And to think that we have taken our commonality for granted, instead of enjoying it!

Have you ever considered that we would look pretty good too if we had our own makeup artist, hair stylist, personal trainer and wardrobe consultant following us around! Not to mention that our photos would also be digitally altered and enhanced, making them magazine worthy!

These are the people that we sometimes compare ourselves to?!? It takes a lot of work to look that good — and we don't have to! Aren't you glad? There is no "perfect" body, so why do we think ours should be? We would invest our time better in appreciating and accepting our imperfect bodies!

The day I could have used a wardrobe consultant . . .

The clock was moving too fast, and I still was not dressed. After trying on several outfits, I finally decided on one, but I still needed shoes. This was a morning of indecision for me, and shoes were no exception! Narrowing it down to two, I put on one shoe from each pair. Calling out to my husband, I asked him which shoe he thought looked better. I turned around a few times and even hopped on alternating feet so he could see one shoe without the other. I finally agreed with his suggestion (which I do not always do), and we were out the door for church.

Some Sunday mornings were challenging! I breathed a sigh of relief as I settled into my seat and the service began. Just as I reached into my purse to turn my cell phone to vibrate, I caught sight of my shoes. I could not believe what I had done! I had on two different shoes! I must have left my closet in such haste that I forgot to replace the mate to the one I selected.

Oh no! I had already visited with several people once we arrived at church – had they seen? It was too late; I could not go home and grab the correct shoe - although I sure wanted to! Perhaps I could try to conceal my mistake by holding my feet a certain way! Where was that wardrobe consultant? I nudged my husband (after all of these thoughts had raced through my mind) to show him my dilemma! He started to chuckle - and I decided that, given the circumstances and my lack of options, that was what I needed to do too!

Laughter is such a wonderful thing, and it definitely took away the stress I was feeling. Before we left church that morning, I even showed a few of my friends what I had done - so they could chuckle too! I remember my grandmother wearing two different earrings before — and even two different shoes! (Perhaps this was hereditary? No, she was partially blind!) Another good thing about being able to laugh at yourself: you can provide merriment for others, creating stories that will be told and retold for generations to come!

Take some time to read through these next few triggers and apply the counteractions to the ones you can relate to.

ⓣ Negative self-talk

Several years ago I came across a photo of myself, and I don't mind saying that I looked pretty good! The problem was that I did not know it at the time . . . Oh, to look like that again, I mused as I gazed at that photo. I felt the Lord whisper to me, "Too much time has already been wasted; enjoy how you look now." Was this possible? I would like to be able to say that, from that moment on, I never once looked at my appearance in a negative fashion, but I can say that my perspective did begin to change. I seriously wanted to accept this assignment from God, and I knew it would be of great benefit to me.

Women, we need to be encouraged to enjoy the way we look! Instead, most of us fall into the never-being-satisfied group: if we have curly hair, we straighten it; if we have straight hair, we curl it. If we are a blond, we dye our hair; if we have dark hair, we bleach it; and if we have gray hair, we cover it as fast as we can! Isn't it exhausting? And this is just our hair!

[Excerpt from my book *Your Home Matters*]

Most of us are completely unaware of how many times a day we speak to or about ourselves in a negative way. Unfortunately, this can become so familiar to us that we are unaware of the damage that it is doing. And this damage is not confined to us: we model this behavior to our children, and they are so much more likely to follow in the same destructive pattern.

Here are some examples of negative self-talk:

You can fill in the blanks.

"I wished I didn't have _____."

"I can't believe I did this again — not again!"

"I am so_____ (or such a _____)."

"When will I ever learn?"

"This is never going to change."

"If only I looked more like _____."

"I might as well give up."

"I can't do this anymore."

That last statement is the only one worth considering: "I can't do this (talk negatively about myself) anymore!"

[Another excerpt from *Your Home Matters*]

C Counteraction: Replace negative with positive

Become aware of when you are engaging in this destructive behavior, and replace the negative statement with a true and positive one. When you do this, you are making it your new habit, and eventually you will feel grateful for who you are and how you look!

I think this true story will encourage you and convince you that this is possible!

A very clever woman I knew several years ago was having a hard time coming up with an anniversary present for her husband. Finally, after much deliberation, she knew exactly what she was going to do. Digging through her Christmas decorations, she found what she needed to carry out her plan and complete his gift.

After enjoying a nice meal out with her husband, she quickly disappeared when they returned home. She needed to place the finishing touches on her gift! Her husband was quite surprised when she appeared before him with nothing on except a big red bow!

She confidently shared this story in a marriage class I was attending. (Fortunately, it was a for-women-only class!) Several of us younger wives were trying not to look shocked - especially after someone had just shared that during intimacy she insisted that the lights be turned off! This brave woman was quite a bit older than us and had lost her girlish figure. I think she was one of those people who thought, just stick a "red bow" on something and it will look great and make a wonderful gift for someone. Obviously she was right; she had been quite confident that her hubby would be delighted – and, in her words, he was!

I never forgot this story, and probably no one else in class did either! It wasn't the red bow that caught my attention (although that seemed to be a nice touch!) It was her confidence. She, like everyone else in the room, did not have a "perfect body," but she didn't let that dissuade her from enjoying her imperfect one. Her confidence made her beautiful to her husband — and to all of us, too, watching the twinkle in her eye as she told us her story!

t When comparisons turn deadly

We compare things all the time; we compare vehicles before a purchase, software for our computers, the clothes we wear, and even the kind of food we like to eat! (If you're like me, you handle a few tomatoes before finding the one you want to buy.) These are normal and healthy comparisons we make on a daily basis.

Comparisons can turn deadly, like when we compare ourselves to others, finding faults with ourselves and no flaws in the others. When we compare ourselves with others, we are usually comparing our faults and failures to their assets and successes. No wonder we come up short — anyone would! So how do we know when are making a lethal comparison? That's easy: It's when how we look, how we feel, and how we get things done make us want to be like someone else, instead of embracing who we are!

ⓒ Counteraction: Consider yourself the masterpiece that you are!

Because God created each of us with unique personalities and unique physical characteristics, we could start considering ourselves masterpieces! Sharon Jaynes, one of my favorite authors, reminds us that it is the fame of the artist that makes a certain work a masterpiece. Her example: we value the art work of our children because we place value on them as the artists.

I am sure you would agree that the whole earth is a magnificent work of art, from majestic mountains right down to a butterfly's wing! God said that everything He created is good! So are you! You are beautiful, and you are one of His magnificent masterpieces! Out of respect for the artists, we would never trash their work, especially in front of them. Without even realizing it, don't we do that to God when we complain about the way we look? Truly each one of us is fearfully and wonderfully made! Just think about how our bodies work, the eyes we have to see, ears to hear, hands to touch, mouths to speak and sing, and tiny taste buds on our tongues to taste coffee! We can start to counteract the trigger of deadly comparisons by believing that each of us is His masterpiece. This is a beautiful way to show appreciation and respect to the artist! I want to remind you to appreciate and show respect to the masterpiece too - that would be you!

ⓣ Feeling the need to impress

In talking with a well-known author, I learned about a dilemma she faced when she and her husband began pastoring a large church. The previous pastor's wife not only had the responsibility for all women's ministry, she did everything very well! The new pastor's wife complained to her husband, telling him that she did not know how to do all of that - nor did she even want to! This sounded like a death sentence to her – besides, she was used to working with a team! Her hubby gave her some wise counsel. He advised her to do what she was expected to do, but to do it poorly! He knew that her talents were in other areas, so carrying out his advice was not going to be a problem for her.

His advice worked! It didn't take the women very long to see that their new pastor's wife really needed their help! Job by job, someone would quietly come alongside of her and say, "I can help you with that – actually, I can do that for you!" In no time at all their women's ministry was running like a well-oiled machine. Most of the women were involved doing what they loved to do, including their new leader! She taught them with excellence; that was her part. She also made everyone feel important - because she knew they were all important to the team!

It was humbling!

I had the privilege of directing a large women's ministry at our church. I soon realized that, to do my job effectively, I had to let go of many of the tasks I was personally doing. I have to admit that it was humbling to watch other women take on each task and do a much better job than I had been doing! I don't know why some leaders feel that they need to do so many things by themselves. Sometimes it is a control issue, and sometimes it's because we think that no one else would want to do the job! It was both for me! I could relate to the story I just told you, although there is difference between her story and mine: I did like being involved in all of the aspects of this ministry.

It was painful as God began to show me that, deep down, I was trying to impress the women with my wonderful array of skills and that I was a bit of a micro-manager — well, quite a bit! It was in God's kindness that He showed me this, because I had the opportunity to change. Teamwork is a wonderful thing! Everything was getting done and with excellence, and new ideas were being implemented too! My job became so much easier because I could concentrate on being their leader and their number one cheerleader!

Ⓒ Counteraction: Recognize your need for others, and appreciate them while you're at it!

In most organizations 10% of the people do 90% of the work, and then they complain about not having help! To counteract the need to impress, don't try to do it all! Allow others to help you — and be willing to help others, giving the credit to them. Like every other counteraction, this is not easy! But it is well worth it.

There is something so freeing when we drop the need to impress others. Having nothing to prove is probably the best thing about it! It's worth mentioning here that sometimes — if there is no one to do the job — maybe it doesn't need to be done. When we run ourselves ragged trying to impress others with all that we are doing, we might not be doing what we are supposed to be doing! And it's safe to say we probably aren't enjoying it either!

🜂 Lack of confidence

I dearly loved my mom, but there were a few things that she said to me as a child that I did not love! One of them was that she often referred to me as "normal." OK, normal should be good, right? My sister was really smart (first child), and I guess you could not have more than one smart child, so my brother and I were described as normal. At least I had company with my brother in this description. Unfortunately, I never asked him if the label of being "normal" plagued him like it did me. Now I'll never know, because he has passed away.

I know that my mom was not out to undermine my confidence, but nevertheless I picked up on the idea that "normal" was not good, and I let it cripple my thinking. I worked very hard in school, and I was rewarded with average grades. My parents never ridiculed me for my average grades, but they never praised me for my effort in receiving an over-the-top grade either.

Something happened to me in third grade that would seal the deal in thinking that I was not smart! Our teacher quizzed us on the capital cities in the United States, and as a class we were having a grand time shouting out our answers — which was something we were rarely allowed to do. She would say the name of the state, and we would shout out the name of the capital city. When my teacher said with great enthusiasm "Oregon" (which was the state we all lived in), I answered back with equal enthusiasm, "Portland!" The room was silent for a moment, and the look on the teacher's face told me two things: one, she felt very bad for me, and two, I was wrong!

Now Portland, Oregon was where I was born and lived until I was married. I knew that Salem was the capital. I had even been to the capitol building before; I just forgot. The silent room quickly filled with laughter — at my expense! It was with crimson cheeks that I didn't remember the rest of our oral quiz — perhaps my answer brought it to an abrupt end. I'm pretty sure, thinking back to that fateful day, that it took our dear teacher quite a while to gain control over our class again.

This defining moment made me feel like I was not even normal, as my mom had always described me. After that incident, I never, ever volunteered an answer to any question again. If an answer was required of me, I would answer with uncertainty, even if I was sure I had the answer right. Something started to die in me that day — my confidence. I began to believe that I really was not very smart, and I took a huge step backwards, no longer believing that I could accomplish anything I wanted to do!

It was only recently that I — once and for all — addressed this hurtful incident in my life and finally gained freedom from it! It wasn't answering a question with the wrong answer that affected me in such a detrimental way; it was being laughed at by my peers. I so desperately wanted to feel accepted by them and my teacher. What I heard when my mom said that I was normal was that I was not smart, and this incident confirmed that to me. If I just keep my mouth shut, no one will know if I don't know the answer — this became my new policy. I'm sure that this, along with other tweaked perceptions I gathered along the path of growing up, made me feel like I needed to be perfect.

Ⓒ Counteraction: We have nothing to prove!

The sooner you can learn to reject feeling like you have to be right all of the time, the better! Just as nobody is perfect, no one is right all of the time either! When we feel the need to prove that we are right, it is our insecurity that is talking. Thinking back to that fateful day, I am sure there were other wrong answers that had been shouted out — and a confident kid would have taken that in her stride, and maybe even have laughed at herself too.

Perhaps we should all practice (when no one can hear us, of course!) saying "I don't know"! It's something most of us do not like to admit. I find it refreshing and quite admirable when someone in a meeting or a group says "I don't understand" or "Can you give me an example? I want to make sure I get what you are saying." If we don't have to be right, our confidence is not threatened when we are wrong.

It doesn't matter how old you are, there is still so much to learn! The ability to continue to learn new things is one of the things that keeps life exciting!

In this chapter . . .

We were reminded that when we are done with negative self-talk, refuse to compare, and drop the need to impress, our confidence will get the boost it needs to steer clear of perfectionism!

In the next chapter . . .

I will tell you about some of the less than perfect places we have called home. But what I am really excited to tell you is the ways I discovered to enjoy right where I was living more than I ever thought was possible, by remodeling just one thing!

CHAPTER 4

If you are comfortable in your home,
your guests will be too!

~ *Sue M. Wilson*

Enjoying Our Imperfect Homes

The house came into view as we drove up the driveway; it looked like they were in the middle of a remodeling project. Feeling familiar with all aspects of remodeling, I was excited to see what their plans were, and I thought this was why our family wanted us to meet their friends. A lot of people ask Len for ideas or his opinion about their home projects, so I was prepared for the same. I felt perplexed as we stepped over boards, making our way to the front door, when I realized that the lumber had been sitting there for quite some time.

Our host and hostess greeted us with great enthusiasm as we maneuvered our way around a few more obstacles into their kitchen, where we were promised a cold glass of freshly squeezed lemonade. Len was quickly summoned, not for his building advice but to reach the pitcher that would hold our drink — he was tall; our hostess was not! We were then invited to take a seat at their dining room table - that did not have even an inch of free space on it. That was not a problem, as our hostess in one sweep cleared a space for all of our glasses. Much to her delight, as she was clearing some space, she found an item that had been lost for who knows how long — her words!

These folks were delightful — and very interesting, to say the least. Our hostess was an artist and wanted to show us some of her work. My sister-in-law and I followed her from one end of her house to the other, viewing her beautiful art that was in almost every room. The paintings were all different and very good! I soon forgot about the possible remodeling project that was not happening and the disarray that her home seemed to be in and just enjoyed this amazing woman — and her art work!

Just before I fell asleep that night, I realized several interesting things about this unique woman. No excuses were made for the mess; she was a very confident woman! She probably could sell her art work if she wanted to. However, the thing that made the biggest impression on me was that, because she felt very comfortable in her home, so did we!

In this chapter . . .

My goal is to help you see your present home through new eyes, so you can start enjoying it like never before! In the world of HGTV and Pinterest, it is easy to focus on our less than perfect homes - and on all of the changes that we would like to make. Discontentment can feel like we are on a runaway train which is impossible to stop.

The way not only to enjoy our homes more but also to feel content living there is to remodel our attitude! I know that can be one of the most painful types of remodeling, but it is totally worth it!

I will share with you a few rules for reigning over perfectionism that I am learning to live by; they insure that I am going to win the war on perfectionism – one battle at a time! Before we get to that, I want to tell you a little bit about our nomadic lifestyle.

Home sweet home - wherever it may be!

Although they all are different, there is a place for each of us that we call home. Some of us can count on one hand how many places we have lived in — and for some of us there aren't enough fingers or toes! I am in the latter group. Being builders, we are drawn to a house that needs a lot of help. Once the remodeling is complete and our home is one of the nicest ones on the street, we start thinking about planting a for-sale sign in the yard! Although this type of occupation lends itself to a nomadic life style, I have to admit that it is very rewarding when someone buys one of our homes and enjoys what we have created! However, getting there was not easy, especially when I was dealing with perfectionism!

Because Len and I have called so many places "home," with several of them fitting into a non-conventional description, it's hard to know where to start! So I'll just jump in! We became home owners at the age of nineteen, buying a fixer-upper in White Rock, British Columbia, and have continued in this pattern for over forty-five years!

To show off his handiwork, Len was forever taking guests back in to a closet or another remote place in our home that no one sees. Because of my pride and the spontaneity of Len's home tours, I felt the need to keep every area of our home perfect all the time! No luxury of tossing clothes or towels on a chair and undies on the floor — heaven forbid! I realize that everyone occasionally has an unmade bed and clothes tossed instead of hung up, but my pride kept me from ever living like that.

I still prefer my bed to be made and our clothes returned to their hangers, but I no longer come undone when that does not happen — and that feels so good! I have become a weekend slob; and I have come to realize that this is an important part of my recovery from perfectionism!

Progress

Unfortunately, back when I was in the throes of perfectionism, whenever I was in someone's home that, in my humble opinion, could use some tidying up, I would think to myself: if I could just have 15 minutes, I could make this place so much better! It's true; I am quite proficient at organizing and making an area of any home highly functional. I even wrote my first book about it. I knew perfectionism was becoming a thing of the past for me when, in a home like that, I no longer felt any compulsion to tidy up or organize something. I could sit at the counter, even if it had to be cleared off to find room for my coffee cup, and enjoy the people who lived there. Freedom!

Here are some rules for reigning over perfectionism and enjoying these imperfect homes of ours!

Rule for Reigning over Perfectionism #1
Be comfortable in, and with, your home!

What if you don't like your home? I have been there too many times to count! My husband is a very good salesman; he can sell me on something I really don't want to do, and temporarily moving into a little beach shack was one of them! We were negotiating on some property six blocks from the beach in Huntington Beach, California. There were two lots, one with a little beach shack on it and the other with a one-room shack that had previously been used as a studio.

Len explained that we could make that little "house" so cute! (He called it a house; I called it a shack!) We could live there, he went on to explain, while we built our new home on the lot with the one-room studio on it. I was having a hard time trying to visualize our young family living there, and I really didn't want to!

Len continued to tell me that our boys could have the attic for their room, and it would be fun for them to climb the ladder that was attached to the wall to get there. Our daughter could have the room they would have to enter to reach the ladder. And best of all: we could comfortably live there while we built our new home on the lot next door!

He finally talked our realtor into selling us the property (it was his) — and selling me on this great plan. Sorting everything out, we seemed to be making it work. Our king-size water-bed did fit as promised, but we only had a foot on each side to get in and out of it. I don't even want to remember how I changed the sheets, but I do remember it involved some awkward movements and a lot of stretching!

We even had house guests!

Both of our nephews (at different times) asked if they could live with us (!?). My nephew lived with his buddy in the one-room studio on the lot where we were going to build, and they were happy as clams. They both worked for Len and could literally roll out of bed and jump in his truck each morning! Len's nephew lived with us after we had started construction on the new house. We had already torn down the one-room studio, so he got to sleep on the couch! He didn't seem to mind!

Family was one thing, but I resisted Len when he wanted to invite friends over for dinner — every time he brought it up. Besides, where would we put them in our kitchen-plus-laundry-room combination? I tried to convince him that there would be plenty of time to have people over for a meal once we moved into our nice new home!

Shortly after pleading my case, I felt a heart-nudge from the Lord.

"You don't know what tomorrow holds; you may never move into that new home."

"I do not like where this conversation is going, Lord," was my immediate response.

I kept trying to dismiss this dreaded thought that I knew was true: I didn't know what tomorrow would hold.

With this new determination I realized that, if I placed my life on hold until this or that happened, my life would always be on hold. I soon made some phone calls — and we would have a full house on Friday night for homemade pizza! We somehow managed to make room for everyone too, with two willing kids sitting on the washing machine and the dryer. They seemed to enjoy the non-conventional dinner-seating as they balanced their plates on their laps. I couldn't help smiling as I looked around the room, with every seat taken and the laundry area occupied too. Our friends were enjoying being in this little beach shack, our new home!

Rule for Reigning over Perfectionism #2
Transitional homes are still home, and they can be a fun place to live, no matter how long you live there!

I am happy to report that we moved from that little beach shack into the new home that we built. Being true to form in the life of a builder (and his wife), after living in this beautiful new home for just a few years, we were ready to build another one on the lot next door. That was the plan! Life is full of risk, and we have taken our fair share of them, but building a new house without selling the one we were living in was not one we were willing to take. The real-estate market can spiral downward, even in sunny California, and the thought of two mortgages scared us spit-less.

Inconvenience or adventure . . .

It didn't take too long for our house to sell or for our new living situation to take shape. Len had been talking to one of our back-alley neighbors, who suggested sub-letting a concrete pad and a bit of ground behind his house from him; he would sub-let it to us for one hundred dollars a month!

"You have got to be kidding me!?!" I said, well knowing this decision would mean either inconvenience or another adventure, depending on who you were - Len or me!

Len replied, "This will be fun! We can go RV shopping and then use it for camping later, once we move into the house!" Funny how one thing can lead to another: I knew he always wanted an RV!

Carefully selecting a thirty-three-foot travel trailer, we were set — well almost. We had a nice bedroom in the back of the rig for us, and Angela, our daughter, could have the fold-out couch in the front, with overhead cupboards for her clothes. But where could we put our rambunctious boys, Chris and Errol? My clever husband decided to extend the awning out over the concrete pad. He then quickly built some paneled walls, carpeted the floor, added a door - and voilà!: a bedroom to die for. Well, that was true, but only for boys!

It is humbling at best when the people you sell your house to discover that you are still their neighbors — you just live in an RV, in the alley right behind them! I explained (perfectionists feel the need to explain or justify what they are doing - remember that trigger?!?) that our unusual living situation would make building our new home on the lot next door more convenient. I failed to mention to them, because of my pride (after all, this was Southern California!), that the money we would save with our cheap rent was the biggest motivating factor!

What if we were breaking the law?

I worried that we might be breaking the law too! My fear was about to be realized as I answered a knock on the door — which was in the boys' bedroom! I had to do some fast talking that day when the city inspector came out to check over our construction progress. Before he left, he realized that we were actually living in the RV that was parked in the back alley, at the back of a house that our neighbor was renting - you can see the complexity of the situation!

"Ma'am, you can't live in the alley!" the inspector said in a gruff voice.

I sensed some compassion in his gruffness and told him, as fast I could spit it out, that this was temporary, and that I didn't like it either! (However, it did keep us close to the construction site, which was a good thing because I wanted to get this job done as fast as possible!) He finally drove away, but only after making me promise that I would nag my hubby both day and night to get our house finished, so we could quit living in the alley — ASAP! Humbling!

Blessing or curse - no pun intended!

Because the beach lots where we lived were long and narrow, you were in close proximity to your neighbors on both sides — not as close as San Francisco houses, but 6' was not much distance! This presented a problem: our neighbor on one side had a vulgar mouth — he wasn't unkind; it was just the way he talked — and he was loud too!

It was annoying hearing him while we were working on the construction of our new home, and I was kind of dreading moving in because of it. Our kids heard words they had never heard before — yikes, I did too! I was on pins and needles when friends would stop by to check out our construction progress, hoping our neighbors were not home.

I shared my concern with one of my friends when she stopped by. Her response was not what I expected: she told me that she was going to ask God to bless us through these neighbors. I was not as enthusiastic as she was; I was just hoping they would move!

Answered prayers

I didn't have the conveniences I was used to while living in the alley in our RV during construction! Early one morning, that same neighbor waved to me as he was backing out of his garage. He seemed surprised to see me loading mounds of dirty laundry into my car. As I waved back, I guessed that he had never seen so much dirty laundry before. That night he knocked on our door. Handing me a set of keys to their house, he mentioned seeing me load our laundry in the car; he then told me that he and his wife wanted me to use their washer and dryer until we moved into our new home.

I tried to give reasons why I could not do this, but he was not hearing it! He reminded me that both he and his wife were gone from 6 a.m. to 7 p.m. all week, and that it was not necessary for me to go to a laundromat when there was an unused laundry just waiting for me. Again, humbling!

I did feel uncomfortable being in their home while they were not there, but it sure was nice to be able to stay near the job site in case subcontractors — and our favorite inspector — dropped by! Grateful to give up the laundromat scene, it wasn't until several weeks later that I remembered the crazy prayer my friend said she was going to pray! Yes, our neighbors did become a blessing to our family, and, yes, he still cursed like a sailor!

One more humbling experience I remember while living in this non-conventional place we called home: I spotted Billy's mom in the grocery store. After asking how the building project was coming along, she told me that her son, best friend of my son Chris, had told them at dinner that their family should move out of their house and into a RV — because it was so cool! I'm usually not at a loss for words, but I didn't quite know what to say to that!

Rule for Reigning over Perfectionism #3
Be willing to share your imperfect home. Don't miss out on a whole lot of fun!

Both Len and I enjoy having groups in our home. But I have to admit that I was ready for a break after hosting our Life Group for several years. The problem had been that the home we were meeting in wasn't always available. Quite often a child, or even one of the adults, was sick, or they had to go out of town. This meant that we had to scramble to find a place to meet or had to cancel getting together.

After this had happened several times, I reluctantly agreed to have everyone meet at our home, although we had barely moved in — yes, to another house! ("What's the problem?" Len asked me. "They have a place to sit!") The problem was I didn't feel ready to host! I didn't like the fact that boxes still lined the walls, pictures were not hung, et cetera, et cetera! I lost again!

We invited; they came — and they absolutely loved seeing our progress each week! I would even ask for their suggestions on where to put this and that, and over time I realized that I really hadn't lost — I had won another battle against perfectionism! We felt so comfortable with this group in our home that we soon became family. We even threw a key under the welcome mat if we were going to be out of town so they would always have a place to meet!

Rule for Reigning over Perfectionism #4
Consistently check your motive...

Why do we want to make changes to our homes? Do we feel the need to compete with the neighbors or our families? Or perhaps to keep up with those friends of ours who live and breathe in every new home improvement idea. What used to motivate me to clean a closet was not always enjoying it clean and orderly, and being able to find things as well! Many times my motivation was to have it clean and orderly for when someone was coming over and might look in there! Heaven forbid! It's a closet! Talk about bondage! Pride was my motive!

What you and I decide to do to our homes should make our lives easier and more enjoyable, and be affordable for us! Projects can be fun, even when they don't turn out exactly as planned — which they rarely do. Being builders, Len and I have had the opportunity to build several homes for ourselves. The more we built, the more I have discovered what works for us and what does not work. I have to tell you: we have never built a perfect home!

It has been said that we women are always changing our minds (I'm pretty sure guys do this too), and I guess I am no exception. As soon as the walls were covered with drywall, I'd think about another electrical outlet placement or something I wished we had done differently, or I wanted to implement some new idea I'd just heard about. I knew that there was no way we were going to tear out any of the newly constructed walls, but it was hard for me to accept that these things were not going to be changed.

When competition is my motive, I'm stuck because there will always be another friend who did something incredible to her home or another magazine or television show oozing with amazing ideas.

I am finding out that it is empowering to discover how I can make less than perfect areas in my home work. Many times they not only work, but they work great — and they look great too!

Rule for Reigning over Perfectionism #5
Choose to be grateful.

I have come to realize that all I can change is my attitude toward anything! And when I decide to change my attitude about my imperfect home, I can really enjoy it! I can replace my discontented attitude with contentment when I choose to have a grateful heart.

Unfortunately, changing our attitude is rarely easy, but is worth practicing!

Instead of seeing all of the things that I cannot change about my home, I can start being thankful for my home, period! In some of the places we have lived, I have had to start with the basics to get my gratitude going, like a cozy bed to sleep in, a warm shower, and a place to prepare food.

Once you get started, even if you just have the basics, you will realize, as I did, that we have a lot to be thankful for! I am a lot more fun to live with too — and to that my family says amen!

Rule for Reigning over Perfectionism #6
It really doesn't matter what people think.

My hubby has a saying that used to make me bristle: "It will look good from the highway!" I have come to realize that not everything we do has to be executed with excellence! Breaking away from perfectionism and its deadly grip does not mean that we have to lower our standards, but having a realistic view of what is necessary — and what is not — will keep us sane! Sometimes we only have the time to do a passable job, and that's OK. At those times it can feel pretty good to actually say, "The job is done!"

Tonya started to giggle as she offered a helpful tip to a group on how to get ready for company in a hurry! You see, she panicked when her college roommate was unexpectedly on the way to her house during a layover at the airport. Tonya estimated that they had about twenty minutes until her arrival. Enlisting her husband, they started from opposite ends of the house, stashing everything that needed to be put away . . . in the bathtub — and then they pulled the shower curtain shut!

When the doorbell rang, they were ready — but a little out of breath! They knew her former roommate would want a tour of the house they had just built, so they obliged. Tonya told us that she was feeling guiltier by the minute as her former roommate commented on how beautiful and tidy their home was! She was curious how this was possible with such a big house and with two small children!

Reluctantly Tonya led her back into the master bedroom and pulled the shower curtain open! After a huge gasp, uncontrollable laughter took over from both Tonya and her former roommate!

A tag line to this story: Tonya told us that it took them several weeks to find things — and she still wasn't sure they got everything put away! My takeaway: Tonya was willing to reveal her secret not only to us, her peers, but to her guest. How freeing was that?!? We all took home a new tip that day, and we silently wondered if there was a way to temporarily lock a shower curtain — only in the case of an emergency, of course!

Len and I had the opportunity to live in our garage/shop while building one of our homes in North Carolina. After we got settled in, I told him that this was probably going to be one of the most fun places we had ever lived in! Because we had a lot of space, we really enjoyed hosting many events while living there too. I loved watching our friends' responses when they walked into this place we called home!

While attending a women's ministry meeting to assist us in getting to know each other better, each attendee was asked to share something unique about herself. I told them I lived in a garage! I felt true freedom in sharing this because I was not embarrassed about it, nor did I feel the need to explain! One of my biggest blessings from calling this place home was learning that it really doesn't matter what people think! I can't tell you how much time I have wasted worrying about what other people think about what we are doing. Why make life harder than it is by feeling the need to explain or justify ourselves? Just go with it — and enjoy it — because it is perfectly imperfect.

In this chapter . . .

I sincerely hope that you have felt encouraged to enjoy your home, no matter where it is or what it is like! I hope too that the "rules for reigning over perfectionism" have resonated with you. Review them often (like I have to), especially when you are feeling challenged to enjoy your imperfect home.

In the next chapter . . .

Whether it is with a spouse, children, extended family or a friend, relationships can be challenging! We will discover how to enjoy our imperfect relationships and detect a few more perfectionism triggers and how they play out in our relationships. We will also find some simple steps we can take to navigate relationships with difficult people.

So get ready for some great changes that will benefit you — and all of those people you are in relationship with too!

CHAPTER 5

*When you stop expecting people to be perfect,
you can like them for who they are.*

~ Donald Miller

Enjoying Our Imperfect Relationships

My pastor reminds us often that there is no "perfect" church because people like us (he included himself) attend them! That is the same reason why there are no "perfect" relationships, not with people anyway. You probably would disagree if we were talking about you and your dog; your dog loves you no matter what you do! But you can't have a relationship — at least like the ones we will talk about in this chapter — without people!

And remember too that we need to approach all of our relationships knowing that grace will be required!

You never know . . .

I was caught completely off guard when a woman timidly approached me with an odd question. "What have I done to make you made at me?" she asked. It seemed odd because, although we attended the same church, I barely knew her. She explained that every time she smiled at me or tried to get my attention, I would turn my head and look the other way. I was completely caught off guard. My heart went out to this dear woman as I tried — the best that I could — to reassure her that I was not mad or upset with her — not even a little bit! It must have been coincidence that I turned my head and did not see when she would smile or wave at me. The really sad part about this story is that she waited several months before approaching me. Yikes! Relationships are challenging enough with the people we do know!

We can offend others even when we don't mean to, like I did to that woman I barely knew! And sometimes — for instance, when we are having a very bad day — we might not care if we are offending someone!

In this chapter . . .

We will talk about our relationships in a marriage and with children, extended families and friends. We will also talk about difficult relationships too - you know, with those sandpaper people who seem to always rub us the wrong way. (We all have them — and sometimes we are them!) I will share several simple things we can do that will help us navigate even the most difficult relationships instead of sabotaging them.

Before we get to that, let's look at a few more triggers and how they affect our relationships.

🕇 Having unrealistic expectations

Unrealistic expectations will sabotage any relationship. Not having them can be particularly challenging for the perfectionist. We talked about having unrealistic expectations in Chapter Two, "Enjoying Our Imperfect Lives"; in this chapter we will take a closer look at what makes an expectation unrealistic.

An expectation is something we hope for or anticipate happening. When we add the word unrealistic to our expectation, we are anticipating something that is impractical, idealistic, and unlikely to happen. Although these definitions are straightforward, our life experiences contribute to what we believe. And what we believe will become what we expect or hope for.

An example of an unrealistic expectation that has developed through life experience could be that you will win the lottery! When your family has placed confidence in eventually purchasing the lucky ticket, or you know someone who won, you believe this is possible for you! Although this might happen, it truly is a long shot.

I have never expected to win a lottery before, but I have unrealistically expected to win the lottery in relationships. I hoped that everyone would like me (remember the people-pleaser trigger?) and want to be my friend! While I was attending grade school, it didn't take too long for my hopes to be dashed. But that didn't stop me from trying.

Along with trying to be perfect myself, I hoped to find perfection in my relationships too. At the time I didn't realize that I was trying to offer myself as a perfect spouse in my marriage, a perfect parent to my children, a perfect relative to my extended family and a perfect friend in friendships. My expectations were unrealistic, and I found disappointment!

When we place unrealistic expectations on ourselves or on others, we are miserable, and so are the people around us. This trigger will set you up for feeling frustrated and for failing in enjoying your relationships.

ⓒ Counteraction:

Be realistic when it comes to all expectations. As mentioned in Chapter Two, all of our expectations need to be tempered with reality. My reality is: not everyone will like me or want to be my friend. Accepting this reality has brought freedom along with a surprising discovery; in time some unlikely people have become dear friends. When I remove "unrealistic" from my relationship expectations, I am free to be my imperfect self. I can also truly enjoy my imperfect relationships!

🅣 Looking to others to make me happy

Another way to sabotage relationships is to concentrate mainly on what you need or want. Perhaps your attention is here because the people around you just don't deliver. That could be true, but if you have several relationships that seem lacking, it's probably because of where your focus is; after all, you are the common denominator.

If you're single, it is easy to be on the lookout for someone who will make you happy (you know, the perfect mate). And if you do find that special person, it won't take too long before you discover that he or she is not perfect after all.

🅒 Counteraction:

We are all in charge of our own "happy." This understanding empowers us to bring health to our relationships. Just like our checkbooks, all relationships need to be balanced. When we continue to make withdrawals without making deposits, we are in trouble! The same is true with our relationships. When we try to extract our happiness from others, our relationships will be in the red.

You also need to make consistent deposits of happiness into your own account. Taking time for yourself and discovering what makes you happy (and actually doing it) will pad your relationship bank account. Take some time to determine and do what fills you up; perhaps it is a hobby, a sport, or spending time outside.

🅣 Criticizing others

Perfectionists don't always limit criticism to themselves; they quite commonly extend disapproval or find fault in others as well. When we are looking to find fault in someone, unfortunately we will usually find it!

My criticism of others can quickly devolve into my judgment of them, without any consideration for the circumstances they are in. Sometimes I criticize people because I can identify with their faults, diverting the attention away from my own shortcomings.

Sometimes it is necessary to assess a situation or what someone is doing, to evaluate if we believe it is right. But that does not mean we need to "criticize" or "judge" the person.

Are any of us truly qualified to become someone's judge? "The one without sin among you should be the first to throw a stone at her." This was Jesus' response to the "religious people of the day" who wanted to stone a woman they caught in the act of adultery. Jesus made it perfectly clear that no one was qualified to stone her. He was the only one who was qualified.

Instead of stoning her, He showed her mercy and grace when He said, "Go, and from now on do not sin anymore." You can read the story in John 8:2-11.

⊙ Counteraction:

In breaking free from perfectionism, I no longer want to criticize myself; and thank goodness that I no longer desire to criticize others either! Although this is no longer my desire, occasionally I still catch myself slipping into criticism and fault finding. When this happens I say to myself (sometimes out loud!), "I don't want to judge!" This action might seem simple, but when it is spoken from the heart, it is not simple; it is powerful!

Keep these triggers and their counteractions in mind as we consider some of our common, imperfect relationships.

Marriage

Please don't skip over this section on marriage if you are single. Even though you are not currently married or perhaps have no desire to be, you can apply the principles and examples to any relationship — roommates included!

My husband Len and I were married at a young age. I think it is safe to say that we continued to grow up together. We were both headstrong and opinionated; we knew exactly how we should live our lives — as husband and wife. We were also confident that we could change the other person to better fit our notions of the perfect spouse! OK, I can hear some of you chuckling. I didn't realize at the time that this is a common fallacy for newlyweds. And it has taken me years to realize that I was the only person I could change!

When two people have been raised in different homes and start life together under the same roof, it should not be a surprise that challenges and heated arguments are normal! During one of these "heated moments" (OK, we were having an argument), Len shouted, "I guess if we are stuck with each other for the rest of our lives, we might as well start having some fun!" I replied just as loudly, "Well, all right then!"

It is funny thinking back on that argument now, but it wasn't funny then.

Some people (who obviously don't know us very well) think we have a perfect marriage! When I share this story, it is usually received with relief — because no marriage is perfect.

Are you one of those people?

One Sunday a few of us were talking about the challenges of marriage. Gil told us what a woman had once said to him: she wished that her husband would show her the affection that Gil showed his wife. He responded with a quizzical look and explained that he and his wife had had a fight on their way to church, and he was desperately trying to get back into her good graces before the service ended!

It's easy to be one of those people who think that other people have a much better relationship than we do, or that they are always affectionate toward one another, or that if we were married to someone like that, our marriage would be wonderful. None of these is true!

The truth is . . .

The people we know who have a good marriage work hard to maintain it. Sometimes we see them working at it, but most of the time we don't. Most of the work is done by showing grace, offering forgiveness, being unselfish, and showing love, even when we don't want to!

We had to laugh when a man we know was being congratulated on his marriage of 60 years. Holding up his hand in the stop position, he said, "You better not congratulate us just yet. It hasn't been going very well lately!" I quickly glanced over at his bride and saw her rolling her eyes!

Obviously he was joking, but he made a fair point: isn't it easy to take the current temperature of our marriage too seriously? Temperatures change, and, chances are, tomorrow you might not feel so upset about a situation. I don't like it when Len tells me that very thing. I don't like it because it is usually true, and because sometimes I just want to be mad for a while! (During those times, he just gives me a wide berth!)

Time well spent

Spending more of your time and effort on being the right person instead of trying to find the right person — or trying to make your spouse the right person — is always time well spent! Concentrating your effort on self-improvement will often bring about a change in your mate. It is like reaping from a harvest of good seed you have sown. A word to the wise: just like a "watched pot never boils," don't spend time looking for results; just make sure you are sowing a bountiful supply of good seed. Results will come, probably when you least expect them to.

A wise woman said that if we could pick and choose the attributes we wanted in our mates, we wouldn't want them! I was not so sure I believed her, but I eventually understood what she meant. I remember arguing about something to do with the Christmas tree before we brought it into the house one year. After storming back into the kitchen, I mused that Len was right — and he looked pretty cute with that stubborn attitude (but I kept those thoughts to myself!). Unfortunately, my heart is not always warmed by his actions, and I'm sure he could say the same thing about me. Why is it so hard to let our mates be right?

It takes team work...

I am thankful that we are different; we make a better team that way. If our thinking were the same on everything, or if we always sided with the way our mate thinks, life would be pretty boring! Disagreements are a normal part of any relationship.

Another way I can keep "team marriage" strong is by not complaining about my husband or sharing his secrets. Likewise, when my husband chooses to not complain about me to others and doesn't share what I have told him in confidence, I know that he has my back. This one simple step will improve all relationships — especially marriages!

Children

From the moment you either conceive or share your plans for adoption, you will most likely encounter people who must share their horror stories with you! This was particularly challenging for me during my first pregnancy. There are already so many unknowns with pregnancy, birth, and adoption — no one needs any more seeds of fear planted in the heart! Raising a family is probably one of the most challenging jobs on the planet, but it is one of the most rewarding jobs too! However, keep in mind that there is no perfect parent or perfect child! (Well, there is one exception: God is a perfect parent — yet look at His children!?!)

Be careful what you say . . .

A word to the wise for those of you who would like to have children but do not have them yet: be very careful about what you say or even think that your children will never do! Talk is cheap and words/thoughts like that can (and most likely will) come back to bite you when you do have a child! Parenting is a humbling experience. I have come to realize that God gave us children to change us! It takes an incredible amount of love, patience, self-sacrifice and humility to raise a child. Learning to choose your battles is key to enjoying any relationship, especially the relationship you will have with each of your children.

First children are encouraged to color within the lines, yet, by the time other children join the family, most parents are just relieved if they don't color on the walls! Our children are not a reflection of us; they are their own people! That doesn't mean that they don't need parenting, they do, but, because no two children are exactly the same, we need to find out what will resonate with each one of them!

Gary Chapman is the author of an excellent book on understanding the love language of others, as well as yourself. The information in *The Five Love Languages* can revolutionize your marriage as well as your relationships with your children, especially teens.

Memories last – make good ones . . .

Spend time making fun memories with your kids. It's not necessary to take them on awesome family vacations, although I'm sure you would enjoy doing that too. Kids will remember the special time you take to just be with them, doing something that you know they like to do — even if it is running through the sprinkler or being a part of another one of those plays they like to put on!

One warm summer night we took our grown daughter and her kiddos out for ice cream. What made this so memorable: we had to get them out of bed to do it! It is too easy (especially for those of us who struggle with perfectionism) to stay in rigid routines. Life passes by too quickly; make time to do some out-of-the-norm things with children (and they don't have to be your children either), and you will be making memories for a lifetime for them — and for you too!

Listen . . .

When her children were little, a dear friend tried to consistently give each of her children a back rub before going to sleep. She discovered that was a good time for them to talk about their day — and the longer they talked, the longer the back rub! Listen to what your kids are telling you, even when it takes them a long time to spit it out!

It is wise to take time to develop a healthy pattern of listening. When you listen to your children, you are showing them that you place value on what they have to say. When you do that, they will remember that you are approachable. This is crucial when they are teens and need to talk things out. When you are really listening to them, they will know that they can tell you anything, without your judgment.

If you have teens, try not to be shocked at some of the things that they might tell you. They don't need you to fix them or the situation; they just need you to listen. It is amazing how many solutions are discovered when someone has the opportunity to just be heard — especially our kids!

It's never too late . . .

You might be like me and wish that you had started really listening to your kids when they were young. I am sure most of us have regrets, but it is never too late to start doing something good, like listening! I believe with all of my heart (although it might take some time) that, when you start listening, really listening, to your children, they will notice and they will appreciate it!

It is really hard to just listen and not chime in with what you think they should do (and believe me, I am still working on this), but when you do listen, they will appreciate it more than you could imagine! And when you and I get really good at listening, they might just ask us what we think - because they know that they can trust us, because we have shown them respect by listening to what they think.

Learn from my mistake!

I wish I had discovered sooner that every individual is in charge of her and his own happiness! When we moved to Australia, my natural urge to encourage propelled me into trying to make each of our three children happy, and adjust to our move better. I would point out all of the special features of this new place we were living in. When that didn't seem to be working, I started comparing our new country to our previous one. I think this made them feel that it was not OK to miss anything from home. My biggest mistake was taking on the weight of their homesickness, which made it impossible for me to deal with mine! I realize now that we all needed to grieve for leaving our previous home and our country, where everything was familiar.

Most transitions are difficult, and ours was no exception, especially during the first few months. I neglected giving ourselves time to adjust. I was worried that moving to Australia had been a mistake. Making mistakes was not something I was yet comfortable admitting! I hope you can learn from mine.

It's hard to see your children struggling, but their character will have a chance to grow through challenging times - just like ours do. We all need a different amount of time to process whatever it is that we are going through. And we all show different emotions when we go through hard times. Some people feel angry and some cry — me, I hold it all together and then I cry! Circumstances don't determine our happiness; our attitude toward them does — and our attitude is something that we can change.

"The days are long, but the years are short."

I wish Gary Thomas and his book *Sacred Parenting* had been around when we were raising our kids. This book was a breath of fresh air to the moms in a parenting class I helped to facilitate. I highly recommend it if you need a boost of encouragement in your parenting. My favorite quote from the book: "The days are long, but the years are short." How true that is! Time with your children under your roof is not going to last forever; choose to enjoy it!

Too many long days?

If you would like to have an empty nest and yet have adult children still living at home, the days might still be l o n g for you!

I want to encourage you to consistently evaluate the situation, making sure that their continuing to live at home is really helping them. When parents provide for their adult children, the children can become handicapped because they never find out that they can make things happen for themselves. We can rob them of the pleasure of experiencing the benefits of hard work too!

Prolonging the inevitable . . .

Sometimes we avoid or prolong the inevitable, which, for our children, is to finish growing up. We all have to do this at some point; we all have to become responsible for ourselves.

Several people doubted that Len and I would make it when we got married because we were so young. With God's help we did make it, though, and we enjoyed feeling like grown-ups . . . because we became them! Although our parents blessed us with many items we could not afford to buy, it certainly felt good when we paid our own way! Allowing children to gradually pay their own way will instill confidence within them and a healthy independence! Try to become their best cheerleader, instead of their enabler!

Extended families

It has been said that every family has some . . . quirky people — and if you don't think your family does, then you are the quirky one! One definition of quirky is "unconventional" — and that's not bad! I believe that we all are quirky in one way or another — and that's OK. In the process of merging two families together, it's pretty easy to see that families are not perfect!. But just because the road can get bumpy, it does not mean that over time you can't learn to enjoy your extended family. Accepting their quirkiness and yours is a great place to start. This eliminates the temptation to compare families.

It is not a surprise that you usually feel more comfortable with your first family. But there is great value in being willing to learn and to appreciate those who live their lives differently from you. Apples and oranges don't need to compete with each other; they are both delicious fruits to be enjoyed, and they even taste good together in the same salad (to me anyway)! (I probably should have said peanuts and walnuts, because all of our families are a little bit "nutty"!) When we try to view the members of our extended families as quirky but "delightful" individuals, we can enjoy each of them for who he or she is! It is not necessary to compare.

Be Your Self . . .

Learning to relax and to be yourself is of great benefit to you, especially when you struggle with letting perfectionism go. Your words and actions will sometimes be misunderstood — and you will probably misunderstand others' words and actions too. This is a normal part of life, and it doesn't need to rock your world.

In a marriage, especially early on, it is important to approach your extended families as a couple. Decide what you want to do before involving anyone else. Although these decisions can be stressful, you will experience less stress by creating a plan together ahead of time. (It is also a good idea to decide what you do not want to do!) It will take commitment to make time for meaningful communication on your part, but will be well worth it as you make these decisions together.

Make life easy on yourself . . .

Why not make life easy on yourself by not over-extending yourself or trying to make everybody happy? Remember the people-pleaser trigger? Everyone is not going to be happy anyway, so you might as well do what you really want to do in the first place!

It is a challenge to deal with decisions and situations that catch you off guard. You will save yourself a lot of grief if you get in the habit of making no decisions on the spot. Once you regularly check with your mate or your calendar first, people will expect that of you. Making a plan together with your mate — and sticking to it — shows your families that you are an impenetrable couple! You can learn to become proficient at this skill, no matter how long you have been married!

If you are a parent or grandparent, your children and grandchildren will respect you even more when you release them to make their own decisions. Chances are, if you support them in their decisions, they will want to hang out with you even more - because there is no pressure!

If you don't experience difficult relationships in your immediate and extended family, you have learned to love, accept, create boundaries and not take everything so seriously OR you live on an island all by yourself! However, for most of us this can be a real challenge.

Friendships

Most things worth having will require both time and effort. Friendship is no exception. A great friendship doesn't just happen, it is cultivated.

In our mobile society many people are forced to give up wonderful friendships when they have to move. Although social media provides a great way to stay connected to the friends left behind, we also need friends we can physically be with. People who move on a regular basis need motivation to make friends, especially lasting ones. Their effort is commendable because they know that they will have to do it all over again if there is another job transfer.

Ideal friend . . .

I have always found it quite interesting to teach a class on friendship. The first time we meet, I like to have everyone list their top qualities in an ideal friend, either writing them down or sharing with the group.

Consistently, the most common qualities are: loyalty, kindness, love, acceptance, forgiveness, patience, transparency, being fun company, and even challenging me to be a better person. In the Scripture verses found in 1st Corinthians, chapter thirteen (also known as the "love chapter"), several more characteristics of love are found which apply to friendship as well: love does not envy, is not rude or easily angered. Love is not boastful or proud, does not dishonor others, is not self-seeking and does not keep record of wrongs.

Be that kind of a friend . . .

A good rule of thumb is to treat our friends the way we would like to be treated — just as the Golden Rule says in Luke 6:31. So often we spend so much time focusing on what we want out of a friendship that we forget to be the kind of a friend that we want to have! Something happens when we shift our focus to giving instead of receiving: we think about ourselves less and others more and we discover it feels great to be a blessing!

Defended by a friend . . .

While on the subject of friendship, I am reminded of an interesting experience I had several years ago. A new lady at the church I attended had a problem with something she heard me say. She decided to complain about it to her new friend. What she didn't realize was that her new friend, Sandy, was also a friend of mine. Apparently Sandy defended me with great enthusiasm, explaining that the lady must have misunderstood what I had said. When I heard about this, I could only hope that I would be that kind of friend in the same situation!

There is more to this story: I heard this from Ellen, the new girl in town! It wasn't long after her conversation with Sandy that Ellen invited me to meet her for coffee. I was surprised by the invitation but even more surprised by our conversation. Ellen began by repeating what I had said, adding that she didn't like it. Trying to conceal the shock I felt, I listened as she told me how she had gone to Sandy with her complaint; she finished up by exclaiming I was fortunate to have a friend like that!

I tried to take all of this in, before addressing the misunderstanding. I tried the best I could to clarify what I had meant by my comment - not trying to defend myself; Sandy had already done that. Satisfied, Ellen remarked that she should have come to me in the first place and asked for my forgiveness. We both agreed that we were lucky to have a friend like Sandy. Being the direct person she was, Ellen went on to say that Sandy had encouraged her to take some time to get to know me, and that was why she invited me to have coffee with her! I have to tell you in all honesty, I sat there feeling rather uncomfortable, even as we turned our conversation toward our families and her recent move.

There are so many lessons I learned from this experience, let me share some of them with you. Both of these women showed good character; it just took a while to see Ellen's! There is such a temptation to agree with negative comments about someone, which can quickly turn into gossip. Sandy's loyalty was amazing. Ellen, on the other hand, taught me even more! It took courage for her to admit she was wrong and to ask for forgiveness. I was impressed that she had taken Sandy's advice in initiating friendship with me. She cared enough to take time to understand what I had said. She even bought me coffee!

Eventually, I tried to place myself in Ellen's shoes. Over the years I've wondered what exactly about my words had so offended her. I have no idea; but that is not what is important here. I realized how easy it is to be offended by something someone says, especially when you don't know the person.

Farsighted friends

I've heard many of my friends say that they miss their eyes, especially when trying to read small print! I would have to agree, but sometimes when others don't see that well, it can be to our advantage! This thought resonated with me after returning home from an impromptu get-together with some friends. "Yikes!" was all I could say when I took a good look in the mirror at my unkempt eyebrows! "Oh dear," I sighed, getting out the tweezers, "this is such a pain!" Then I had to chuckle: the friends I had just had lunch with all needed their glasses to see the menu; they were farsighted! My eyebrows were safe; my friends never saw them!

Farsighted friends are the best ones to have: you always look good to them! I want to be a farsighted friend too, looking past faults and thinking the very best, because my friends always look good to me!

Difficult people

I have saved this group for last: difficult people. We all encounter them, and sometimes we are them! Fortunately, there are some steps we can take that will make any relationship better — but especially our most challenging ones. By following these steps, we will improve the quality of our lives — even if the other person never changes! Warning: these are not for the faint at heart!

- Change the subject when you sense that it is going somewhere it shouldn't. This can be extremely difficult if one of your "hot buttons" is being pushed!
- Ask questions to find out things you did not know about the person. This will help you to see them in a different light; it is also a great way to direct the conversation away from negativity.
- Look for something good in the person, and focus your thoughts on what you discover.
- Plan ahead to do something that you both enjoy. This will take the attention away from your differences.
- Agree to disagree; not everyone thinks the same way — and we don't have to!
- Include encouraging words in your conversation; they will bring peace with them.
- Determine to speak positively about the difficult people in your life, instead of choosing to gossip about them. This will eventually turn your heart around.
- Pray for them. It is hard to be angry with someone you are praying for!
- Offer forgiveness, especially when they don't deserve it. It is the best gift you could ever give!
- Choose every day (sometimes every hour) to not be offended.

When we practice these steps, we are choosing to travel on the high road. The challenging people in our lives will have to decide for themselves how to respond to us, but that does not have to determine our actions. By choosing to not be a part of the problem, we are also able to live far above the fray — and that is really living!

In this chapter . . .

We were reminded that relationships need work! Investing time and effort in our marriage, relationship with our children, extended family or friends is worth investing in; even those difficult people in our life!

In the next chapter . . .

We will see that it is possible to enjoy our imperfect jobs. We will also talk about how to become either the employee or employer extraordinaire through living by some simple principles. I can't wait to tell you about a friend of mine who was in a job he struggled in and what he did that changed everything!

CHAPTER 6

I used to look for a perfect job.
Now I look for any job and make it perfect.

~ *Owen J. McClain*

Enjoying Our Imperfect Jobs

There is a young man I want to tell you about. He worked hard at a business, but his boss did not recognize his talents or hard work. He applied for other positions as he became aware of them, but nothing seemed to work out. Every day he got up and went to work, and he kept doing all the aspects of his job in a most excellent way, even though his responsibilities seemed to grow daily and were all over the board! He also leaned on the Lord's strength to help him make the best of his situation . . . until something changed.

Well, something finally did finally change — he did! He settled into his job and stopped looking for something better. He made right where he was better! He became thankful that his job provided for his family, even though it barely did. After a while, his boss began to notice and appreciate this man's attitude and hard work. He also saw that everyone who knew this young man loved him and his family.

After deciding to make the best of his situation, this young man eventually met with his boss to ask for a raise. He carefully laid out the details of each area that he was responsible for, and he reminded his boss of his vast job description and his dependability. Their meeting concluded with his request for a raise. He confidently told his boss the salary that he needed to be fairly compensated for his work and to meet the needs of his growing family.

He got the raise — and it ended up being more than he had asked for! His patience and hard work did eventually pay off. I truly believe that, if his boss had not agreed to give him the raise, he would have looked for another job — and found one! He would have been able to leave his job knowing that he had done everything he was asked to do, and even more. You might think that he was being taken advantage of, and perhaps he was, but he had nothing to be ashamed of.

The "perfect" job . . .

If we were in a group together, what you would enthusiastically shout out to describe the perfect job? We probably would all agree that it would be great to have all of our hard work recognized and reflected in our paycheck. It would also be nice to have all the resources we need when we need them and then to have adequate time to get the job done. We would want to have a team around us that not only made us look good (because they recognize genius when they see it) but didn't try to take credit for something that we did! Regular days off, a flexible schedule, and paid vacations would be a must, to allow us time to unplug and recharge.

We probably can think of more features and perks that would constitute the "perfect job" and that would make going to work more enjoyable. But would they really? Wouldn't we continue to find things that we wished were different? Let's face it: going to work every day is not always easy. It really doesn't matter whether we work from home or travel to a location — it is still work. As long as we are looking for the impossible and complaining about our work, we will never be able to enjoy the job we have! Because we have established that perfection is an illusion, let's forget about all of those wonderful attributes we just listed and get back to reality!

Is "work" really a bad word?

Unfortunately, many people have negative feelings when they hear the word "work." In jest, some even consider "W O R K" as one of those distasteful four-letter words! Our kids moan and groan when given a chore list. (Actually, I am not even sure if children know what a chore list is anymore!) And we can't believe what our bosses expect of us! It is common to hear stories complaining about how stupid bosses are or bragging about getting away with doing the least amount of work possible and still collecting a paycheck, or of employers complaining about their employees!

When we approach our work with an "us vs. them" mentality (we verses our employers or we verses our employees), our jobs become full of strife and stress, and we don't enjoy them!

In this chapter . . .

You will see seven simple strategies that you can apply to any work situation and that will bring about significant changes in your job, whether you are an employee or an employer. You will discover the great benefits from changing your attitude toward work, just like the young man did in the story at the beginning of this chapter. These strategies can be both modeled and taught to the kids in your life, and that will give them a huge advantage! But most of all, my hope is that in this chapter you will appreciate the work that you do, see the contribution you make, and come to really enjoy it!

Seven simple strategies for enjoying your job:

One — *Develop confidence*

Did you know that God planned good things for us to do before we were even born? How about that for having a purpose in this world! All too often, however, our focus can rest on what we do not do well instead of on honing the skills that we do have. You and I develop confidence when we recognize and utilize our strengths. Oftentimes they are discovered by trial and error! Let's shift our focus onto what we do well, and then settle down and do it!

In the workplace it's easy to think that job security means having to be able to "do it all." I am here to tell you that there are very few, if any, people who can really "do it all." And I would guess that those few who are trying to "do it all" are not doing anything very well. The "do it all" mentality will result in burn-out sooner or later, and it is the confident person who recognizes and appreciates the skills of others. Unhealthy competition, especially in the work place, chips away at our confidence. Competition becomes detrimental when we become jealous of another's ability or wish them harm.

Two — *See the value in team work*

Teamwork is cooperative work or effort with the common purpose to get a job done, bringing benefit to all. This is pretty straightforward in theory but takes time and effort to develop. The place we understand teamwork best is in the sports world. It really doesn't matter what sport it is, we understand that it will take teamwork to develop skills, play well, and win the game!

Sometimes we are wowed by the awesome plays of an individual, but it is always more impressive when we see the entire team work together! When each individual does his job on the team, all those individuals are working together to get the job done — and win the game! I think we all walk away feeling good from those kinds of movies where, win or lose, the team learned to work together. The old adage fits well here: It doesn't matter if you win or lose; it is how you play the game! Obviously, it is a lot more fun to win the game, but probably more character-building lessons are learned from losing!

Truly being able to enjoy another's success is a strategy very few people develop, but when you practice this skill, your confidence will soar, and you will be marked as a MVP!

Three — *Honesty still is the best policy . . .*

As children most of us have heard the phrase "Honesty is the best policy." We also learned there would (eventually) be consequences when we were not honest. As childhood fades, so can our motivation to be honest, particularly in the workforce. With less accountability it is easier to a make a dishonest decision, especially if we think nobody's looking!

Being honest in the so-called insignificant things is significant — and can set us apart from the norm. So is admitting to our mistakes instead of trying to conceal them. As soon as we have done something wrong or something goes wrong, we need to make a bee-line to our boss or supervisor. In going to the boss first, there's is a good chance we will gain his or her respect and that we both can find a solution together. This is not always the case, but, in the long run, it is always better to be known as someone who admits fault and takes responsibility. Yielding to any dishonest behavior can be a determining factor in the length of our employment.

For the business owner dishonesty can be a determining factor in the longevity of the company — especially when it is in construction! There are many negative thoughts that come to mind when we hear the word "builder." Len and I have heard our share of horror stories, and perhaps you have a few of your own. So right off the bat, as a general contracting business, we have to prove ourselves. One of the ways we can do that is by doing what we say we are going to do, instead of yielding to temptation of telling a customer what they want to hear. This is lying when it is not true!

Whether you are an employee or an employer, it won't take long for your honest character to ring true. An honest and reliable reputation will afford you more opportunities than trying to get ahead through dishonest means ever will!

Four — *Treat people the way you want to be treated*

Let's face it: we all like to talk about ourselves, even those of us who consider ourselves introverts! We like it when others care enough to ask what's going on in our life or about our family, instead of just talking about theirs! This is also true in the work place. When we take the time to get to know the people we work with, we show we value them. Employers or employees, we show respect for our colleagues when we take an interest in their individual lives. Taking the time and effort to connect on a personal level makes the workplace easier and more enjoyable too! Showing respect for and interest in others is a wonderful habit to cultivate, one that marks us as thoughtful individuals.

Be wise. No one likes to be gossiped about, right? If you are ever tempted to spread gossip, take a minute to think how you would feel if someone gossiped about you. You can refrain from gossiping in the first place. Be mindful as well not to share personal information with a gossip, because you know what will happen! If someone is always talking about others in a negative way, he or she will probably talk the same way about you.

Five — *Don't be afraid to be generous . . .*

Sowing seeds of generosity as an employer will bring to you a bountiful harvest in loyal employees. Showing generosity brings lasting benefit to you as an employee too! You can be generous with your time, going above and beyond to do a good job or helping a fellow employee. You are being generous when you show interest in others (see the previous section) and when you affirm someone's work.

Another facet of generosity is being able to recognize and appreciate it when it is being shown to you! You are being generous in return when you show gratitude! It is a lonely world out there when your concerns are only for yourself. Generosity in the work place makes any imperfect job more pleasant!

Six — *Moving on*

There are many reasons a job may come to an end, few of which you can control. However, you can control how you leave that job. Leave in the best way possible. If your new boss calls your old boss for a reference, you will be very glad you exited with integrity! When you leave on a good note, even when the situation is not good (especially when the situation is not good), you are setting yourself up for success wherever you go!

Be careful how you arrive at your new job too! If you arrive at a new job still complaining about your previous job, it paves the way for a repeat of what you have just been through! Negative talk about your previous job can make others feel wary of you, especially your new boss.

Hard work eventually pays off. So too does leaving a job in the best way possible: with honesty, integrity, apologies if necessary, and a willingness to learn from the situation!

Seven — *Redefining success*

This last simple strategy will take some time to develop and actually encompasses practicing all of the strategies previously mentioned. All too often our definition of success is not achievable or even rewarding if we did ever reach it! And all too often we define success as being prosperous, up-and-coming, well-off, wealthy, or rich. I prefer the adjectives fruitful, positive, and effective; they have lasting benefit.

Previously, we talked about the dangers of comparison. We usually have particular persons in mind when we think of what being successful looks like. And then we feel completely deflated when we compare ourselves to those others, those "successful" people, because we are comparing our failures to their successes. We probably don't know how many times they have failed (unless they have made this public; I love those stories!) before finally accomplishing what they wanted to. I think they would define success as never giving up! They persisted until they succeeded, and so can we!

In this redefinition process, just remember that a mistake is not really a mistake if you learn from it! There is a "learning curve" to everything. Very few people execute something to their satisfaction the first time they try it. Just as there is basic training in the military, there is a training period in most jobs. Like most of us, you might learn best through on-the-job training, discovering what works — and what you never want to do again!

I used to throw away my failed attempts at something because I did not want anyone else to see them - and because I did not want to be reminded of them. If only I would have taken the time to study my "failure" (like an inventor does), I could have discovered how to make improvements. What a shift in thinking! When we know that we can learn from everything we do, we will have no fear of trying new things! And that, my friend, opens up a whole new world of possibilities!

Fame and fortune are fleeting! The numerous stories about people who won a lottery and then became bankrupt are proof of that! When making money is our main focus, we will never make enough! And as far as fame goes, very few people will be remembered one hundred years from now; I can't even remember who won the World Series or Super Bowl last year! (They must not have been my team!)

To me success is discovering who you are and investing in that. It is also just as important (as you have read throughout this book) to discover who you are not! My definition includes feeling confident in what you do and how you do it. There is great satisfaction, and contentment too, in knowing that you gave your best. That not only feels good it feels right!

In this chapter . . .

You met my friend who changed everything about his job when he changed his attitude. We talked about what a perfect job would look like — and gave that a pass because it does not exist! We discussed seven simple strategies that will set you apart from the norm when you implement them in your job. I hope that you and I can apply the principle in the quote appearing at the beginning of this chapter:

I used to look for a perfect job. Now I look for any job and make it perfect.

(Owen J. McClain)

Let Me Introduce You to Someone Who Actually Is Perfect

I have spent some time making inquiries and discovering facts and even personal stories about people who are of interest to me; perhaps you have too. When we do this, it is not uncommon to begin to feel like we have some sort of a connection with these individuals, although this connection is a loose one at best when we do not personally know them.

Unfortunately my quest for knowing about God was becoming more like a fact-finding mission until I discovered that God desired a personal relationship with me. This changed everything! My desire moved from wanting to know about God to wanting to know God. I also realized that I was created (and so are you) for this very purpose: to know God through a relationship with Him! How is this even possible?!? Jesus, God's perfect Son Who was without sin, paved the way by taking all of my sin (past, present and future) upon Himself at the cross, making me acceptable (and perfect) in the sight of God!

If you have not personally met Jesus, allow me the privilege of introducing Him to you through some of His perfect attributes:

1 John 4:18 God's love is perfect and expels all fear. We need not fear judgment if we accept God's love for us and provision through Jesus.

Isaiah 26:3 God will keep in perfect peace the mind that is fixed on Him. There are all kinds of things we can think about or dwell upon, but when we choose to fix our mind on God, perfect peace is ours!

Psalm 19:7 God's word is perfect and will restore our soul! Restoration is one of God's specialties! Through relationship with Jesus, our relationship with God is restored and eternal life with Him is ours. He also loves to restore our families, our health, and anything else that needs repairing; just ask Him about that!

2 Corinthians 12:9 God's power is perfected in my weakness. He did not create us to walk through life all on our own, to shoulder our cares alone. We can depend on His strength to empower us.

Now that you have been introduced to this perfect one, it is really quite simple for you to enter into relationship with God through Jesus. You just have to tell Him that is what you would like to do. I want to encourage you to begin your relationship by feeling comfortable using your own words, in your own way — after all, He already knows what is in your heart.

I can promise that once you enter into this relationship (or rekindle a relationship you once had with Jesus), your life will never be the same! It will not be easy, but you can trust Jesus to perfect (complete) His love and peace and to restore your life, giving you the ability to believe and to do the impossible – just like He said you would (Mark 9:23)!

By the way, "Welcome to the family!"

Love & Blessings,

Sue

A Note from Sue

I am so proud of you and your determination to break away from the bondage of perfectionism! My hope is that you will enjoy your wonderful imperfect life more than you ever have! Remember: it will take time to develop new habits. Becoming proficient in applying counteractions against any trigger that draws you back toward perfectionism is a habit worth developing. It really doesn't matter how long you have given in to the relentless ways of perfectionism; living free will cause you to never want to live that way again! You've got this! If I can make this transformation, so can you!

I would love it if you would give me a review of this book at Amazon.com. If you would like to contact me directly you can through my web site at www.suemwilson.com

About the Author

Lavender Valley Photography

Sue Wilson grew up in the Pacific Northwest, but during her forty-plus years of marriage, Sue and her husband Len, have called Canada, Oregon, California, and Australia home, before putting down roots in North Carolina.

As custom builders, Sue and Len have enjoyed making a beautiful homes from badly neglected ones. They shared these home-making and home-building adventures with their three children and now are watching them —and even some of their nine grandchildren—with pride and pleasure, in adventures of their own. Since the publication of her first book, *Your Home Matters*, Sue and Len have added seven great-grandchildren to their family!

"My previous years of living in the prison of perfectionism compelled me to write this book. I am grateful to say that I am free from that compulsion and now enjoy life to the fullest – and so can you!"